A Sustainable Presbyterian Future

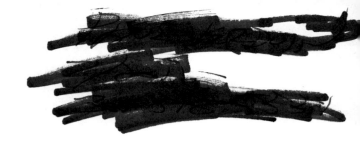

A Sustainable
Presbyterian Future

What's Working and Why

Louis B. Weeks

GENEVA

Geneva Press
Louisville, Kentucky

© 2012 Louis Weeks

First edition
Published by Geneva Press
Louisville, Kentucky

12 13 14 15 16 17 18 19 20 21—10 9 8 7 6 5 4 3 2 1

Scripture quotations from the New Revised Standard Version of the Bible are copyright © 1989 by the Division of Christian Education of the National Council of the Churches of Christ in the U.S.A. and are used by permission.

Excerpts from "American Protestants Today: Thriving, Tottering, and Tinkering Together on the Mainline," *Journal of Presbyterian History* 88, no. 1, is reprinted by permission of the editors.

The graph is reprinted by permission of Research Services, Presbyterian Church (U.S.A.).

Book design by Sharon Adams
Cover design by Dilu Nicholas
Cover art: © Presbyterian Church (U.S.A.)/Presbyterian seal stained-glass window,
Presbyterian Center, Louisville, Kentucky

Library of Congress Cataloging-in-Publication Data

Weeks, Louis
    A sustainable Presbyterian future : what's working and why / Louis Weeks. — 1st ed.
       p. cm.
    Includes bibliographical references (p.   ).
    ISBN 978-0-664-50319-2 (alk. paper)
    1. Presbyterian Church (U.S.A.) I. Title.
    BX8969.5.W44 2012
    285'.137—dc23

                                                2011051718

♾ The paper used in this publication meets the minimum requirements of the American National Standard for Information Sciences—Permanence of Paper for Printed Library Materials, ANSI Z39.48-1992.

Contents

Preface

*I*t is my hope that this book will help us take stock and take heart as Christian disciples in Presbyterian churches.

Our salvation comes by the grace of God. Presbyterians have never claimed, as have some other streams of Christianity, that our church is "God's last and only hope." With a few exceptions, Presbyterians have not offered believers the possibility that anyone can attain perfection in this life either as an individual or in a faith community. In fact, we have been downright modest most of the time. We have been open to the biblical truth, stated by the apostle Paul, that there is "the righteousness of God through faith in Jesus Christ for all those who believe." People are not saved by the church![1]

No Presbyterian speaks ex cathedra or controls our doctrine and practices from a "seat of power" (the meaning of the word *cathedral*). I have, however, heard a few Presbyterians try to do so! Presbyterians have no pope (from the Greek word for father, like *papa*), no one man selected to have that authority, the way Roman Catholic Christians have. Our standards for worship and work in the Presbyterian Church (U.S.A.) teach that God's Spirit "sets us free to accept ourselves and to love God and neighbor . . . binds us together with all believers in the one body of Christ, the Church."[2] Particular churches may be "more or less pure," but even the "purest churches under heaven are subject both to mixture and error."[3] In other words, we know our Presbyterian part of the church, while holy, will always have holes.

This is not a book about how to "fix" the Presbyterian Church. Plenty of those exist already! Some of the "church-improvement" books prove exceedingly helpful, and we will examine congregations using a few of the best of them. Some others appear downright destructive in tone and argument. We will leave them alone.

In this effort to glimpse our current situation, our future prospects, and the resources for vital ministry, we will simply mark several signs along the way—of our identity and culture, our new ecology for faith development, our new ways of connecting, and our defining qualities of life together. Some "best practices" of others we cite may suggest ways to improve congregational or denominational life.

With some hope and openness we can review our current situation and imagine our future prospects. When we are hopeful we do our best work together.

It was tempting in the past for American Presbyterians to be arrogant—to presume that our Reformed way is the best of all ways of being Christian. Time and again, the Bible warns us about pride going before falls, taking places of honor too quickly at banquets, and trying to be "first" in the kingdom of heaven.

Currently, it is easy for us to become despairing—to consider ourselves religious failures because our numbers and our influence in the United States have diminished during our lifetimes. The New Testament letters, such as the Epistle to the Hebrews, speak of holding firm to "the confidence . . . that belong(s) to hope" (3:6). Jesus kept telling disciples "Do not be afraid" (Luke 5:10). Presumption and despair are twin sins against the virtue of Christian hope.

I hope this book will be for you a word of assurance, a word of encouragement, and a word of challenge. I hope the examples from Presbyterian churches and the insights from some people with energy, intelligence, imagination, and love will inspire you to seek excellence in the worship and work of your congregation and, more broadly, in life.

Living in hope, shunning both despair and presumption—that is how healthy Christians seek to live. The Letter to the Hebrews tells us to receive the assurance of hope so we do not become sluggish. Rather we live now as those before us, "who through faith and patience inherit the promises" (6:9–12).

Tottering and Thriving

As you know all too well, these are times of confusing and some-times contradictory realities. We seem to be tottering and thriving at the same time. The membership numbers and the public influence of the Presbyterian Church (U.S.A.) are dwindling, and at the same time hundreds of thousands of Presbyterians are enjoying life in vibrant congregations. We hear that our missionaries number fewer than two hundred, a small percent of the number who served in global missions only a few decades ago. Yet more Presbyterians than ever—perhaps as many as one hundred and fifty thousand of us—took mission trips this past year, many of them to foreign countries. We hear that a great majority of adults in the United States say the Bible is God's Word; but most Christians also cannot even name the four Gospels, much less the Ten Commandments or the Beatitudes. We hear that conservative churches are growing, but we read of the bankruptcy and demise of numbers of such congregations.

In our broader culture, we see the contradictory currents as well. America maintains an energetic democracy while a large number of our citizens "opt out" of political involvement. We have increased our modes of communication in the United States, and we have become exceedingly polarized in many respects—politically, cultur-ally, and spiritually. Increasingly, Americans consider such institu-tions as marriage to be irrelevant, but a recent poll found that almost all Americans respect the family as the major institution in Ameri-can life.[4] A vibrant capitalism spawns new ideas, products, and businesses among us; while the rampant consumerism on which our economy depends seems to dampen future prospects for growth and disciplined attention to long-range challenges.

Insightful, evangelical Christian James Davison Hunter points out these and other indications of competing forces among us: "vitality and lassitude, energy and exhaustion. . . . Not least, the achievements of technology have been stunning, but delivered new forms of violence and oppression."[5] These truths are cold com-fort for those of us who yearn for a faithful, energetic, and healthy PC(USA).

Major "Tinkering" with Our Regulations

At this particular point in our life together, there is particular turmoil. A majority of PC(USA) presbyteries ratified in 2011 two actions from the 219th General Assembly (2010)—that we change the wording of section G-6.0106b (now G-2.0104b) and that we adopt a new Form of Government. We are forever "tinkering" with our form of government, and we have made changes in our *Book of Order* more than three hundred times since we formed the PC(USA) in 1983. But these two changes are significant ones.

The effect of the first change is to eliminate the clause "to live either in fidelity within the covenant of marriage between a man and a woman, or chastity in singleness" (G-6.0106b). Instead, councils are led through the examination process by the more general, "councils shall be guided by Scripture and the confessions in applying standards to individual candidates" (G-2.0104b), a wording similar to that for our first two hundred years. Numbers of congregations have threatened to leave the PC(USA) if the "fidelity and chastity" clause disappeared.

The second ratification is more sweeping, for it seeks to recast the whole governing structure of the PC(USA)—to offer less regulation and more resources for Presbyterians in mission, particularly for congregational leadership in the myriad contexts of service and witness. In the words of the press release declaring the result, "congregations, presbyteries, and synods will have the opportunity to tailor mission and ministry to fit their own particular contexts and challenges."[6] Many conservatives as well as many liberals in the PC(USA) opposed this change, and some predict that chaos and a hastened demise of Presbyterianism will result.

Whatever the long-term consequences of these monumental decisions, in the short term, Presbyterians will be pioneering in new terrains. The new form of government uses a new vocabulary, or rather recalls us to a vocabulary Presbyterians used to employ. So we will be referring to our elders again as *ruling elders* and our pastors as *teaching elders*. (The term *minister of Word and Sacrament* is still recognized as an alternative to *teaching elder*.) We will be speaking of sessions, presbyteries, synods, and our General Assembly as "councils," no longer as "governing bodies," "judicatories," or "church courts." Rather than speak of "the mission of the church," the new Form of Government speaks of "God's mission in the world," which the church is called to serve. Remember, through our councils (General Assembly and presbyteries) we voted to employ these words and explore this terrain together.

So let us look in turn at the indications of doom and some experiences of thriving among us. Let us then consider some of the ingredients in the changing culture of the Presbyterians. Finally and most important, let us name some of the resources that can be employed as we lean into God's future and seek to be disciples worthy of the gifts we have been so graciously given.

Outline of the Argument

We begin in chapter 1 with a brief examination of that confusing "tottering and thriving" situation today and some interpretations of our Presbyterian history. We highlight three lessons from the major study of the PC(USA) twenty years ago: that an ecology, or ecosystem, provides nurture in Presbyterian identity and culture; that Presbyterians in America have been connected and organized in several different ways; and that most members belong first and foremost to their local congregation.

Chapter 2 asks about the nature of our Presbyterian identity and culture. What do we represent within the Christian movement? What marks our life together? What is worth saving? How are we divided and united today?

Chapters 3 and 4 explore our traditional ecology—ways of growing in faith as Presbyterians—and the new ecology of formal and informal institutions that now prevail. Though we mention some of the practices in worship and some of the vehicles for Christian education, we concentrate on the relationships for service, mission, and evangelism.

Chapter 5 offers some observations concerning ways the new ecology affords Presbyterians integrity in worship and work. We describe some of the challenges and characteristics of leadership and service by ruling elders, teaching elders, deacons, and other congregational leaders.

Chapters 6, 7, and 8 examine some of the resources available as Presbyterians leaders help their congregations and councils to thrive in the new ecology. Chapter 6 focuses on congregational resources. Chapter 7 looks at denominational resources. And chapter 8 examines relationships among Presbyterian congregations with Presbyterian seminaries and colleges.

Chapter 9 follows some of the ways Presbyterian congregations are engaging explicitly in evangelism. Many of our congregations are openly evangelical, and others are just learning to tell the gospel story together.

Chapter 10 looks at Presbyterian new church developments and some additional elements that may comprise parts of the new ecology. These issues, sustaining for some Presbyterians and a threat to others, can provoke learning for all of us.

Chapter 11 concludes the study with some evidences of our sustainable future and a prayer that we may be faithful Christians as we embrace God's future.

Research for this project included interviews with scores of Presbyterians, many in positions of denominational leadership as well as service in local churches. Almost nobody expressed a desire simply to maintain the PC(USA), much less to "save" it. The great majority, however, spoke fondly of their churches and of the councils of the PC(USA). Most Presbyterians love their church and respect the contributions of Presbyterians through the years. Some interviewed told of particular aspects of Presbyterian life that are crucial for Christian worship and witness. We will concentrate on those elements of our life together, asking about viability for the future.

Along the way, in every chapter, we seek to learn from glimpses of actual Presbyterian congregations in life together—big churches, little ones, some obviously thriving and others struggling. I term some of these glimpses into local churches "case studies," though the situations do not point to a particular decision confronting the leaders. I hope these cases, and the more succinct illustrations from other Presbyterian congregations, help you make use of the book's insights and ideas. I also hope the use of real names and locations will help Presbyterians and others make connections that can inform work and worship in congregations.

Acknowledgments

I am deeply indebted to scores of ruling elders, teaching elders, scholars, and garden-variety Presbyterians for insights and illustrations and for editing and making constructive suggestions along the way. I began this project making a list of those who made active contributions to my learning and to the manuscript. It grew like topsy, and soon I realized I could not name each person. Sorry. This book represents listening to and learning from several hundred people in scores of congregations over the past twenty years, ever since the *Presbyterian Presence* study.

Many of those named in the book gave freely of their time and talents to read portions of the manuscript and permit use of their words and names. I am deeply grateful to everyone. Perhaps identifying the churches and people by name will lead to conversations and the sharing of wisdom and inspiration. I certainly hope so.

An earlier version of this argument and some of the allusions to Presbyterian congregations appeared first in the *Journal of Presbyterian History*, vol. 88, no. 1, titled "American Protestants Today: Thriving, Tottering, and Tinkering Together on the Mainline," and the material is reprinted by permission of the editors.

Editors David Heim of *The Christian Century*, Jack Haberer of *The Presbyterian Outlook*, Richard Bass of *Alban Institute Press*, and Eva Stimson of *Presbyterians Today* graciously cooperated in publishing materials related to some of the congregations and themes explored. James Lewis and the board of The Louisville Institute provided a grant that permitted much of the travel undertaken for this project, though I still owe them the future book this one interrupted.

I am also grateful to David Dobson, who expressed initial interest in the topic and persisted in support along the way, and to the production and sales team of the Presbyterian Publishing Corporation. Thanks again.

My wife, Carolyn, and other members of the family have been forgiving of my monomania and the interruptions in times together, so I could keep learning and writing about Presbyterian churches and the PC(USA). Thanks!

Louis Weeks
Williamsburg, Virginia

Chapter 1

Presbyterians Tottering and Thriving

Did you see the *Wall Street Journal*?" asks my friend in our Sunday school class. "They had an editorial, 'Where Have All the Presbyterians Gone?' It's pretty devastating."[1]

"Yes," another adds. "Why are we losing so many members? I hear the PC(USA) will be gone by 2060."

"What can be done to turn this thing around?" still another chimes in. "It looks like this congregation will be by itself pretty soon from what I hear. We don't have missionaries in other countries, and all we do here in the United States is squabble."

Here we are in a flourishing congregation, one that has grown significantly in the past thirty years while also giving birth to a PC(USA) new church development nearby with a "loan" of members. Here we are in a thriving Presbyterian church worrying about the death of the PC(USA). Hundreds of PC(USA) congregations are thriving today as we are, some in rural areas and small towns, some in suburbs, some in urban areas. Yet all of us know about other congregations that are languishing, unable to sustain leadership or pay a pastor, many of them deeply conflicted. And some denominational offices and middle councils seem frequently dysfunctional—stuck in ruts of ineffective practices and repeatedly treating divisive issues—while others function more effectively than they did in the 1980s and 1990s.

Where should we begin in addressing these questions and worries?

Over the past decades, I received similar questions and heard the same concerns from Presbyterians and others in every part of the country. Even when visiting Presbyterian churches in Korea, Ghana, and elsewhere, I've heard questions about the PC(USA) and expressions of dismay about the future prospects for the "mother church" that helped them form. Questions about membership, wherever voiced, also carry an underlying concern about the viability, even the survival of any generous Presbyterianism for the future. Worse, pessimism about the prospects for our future can become self-fulfilling prophesies of failure.

Now in retirement, and after fifty years of studying Presbyterian denominations, visiting hundreds of congregations to preach, teach, and learn about their worship and work, and after helping lead major research projects on matters Presbyterian, I can respond with some knowledge and assurance about our situation.

I am deeply concerned about the decline in membership. The PC(USA) officially numbered 3.1 million members in 1983 when it was formed. The two denominations that united to comprise it had both been losing members already. In 1965, those two Presbyterian denominations together had numbered 4.25 million. By 2010, the number in the PC(USA) had dwindled to 2 million—less than half the number of that 1965 high point in number of members.[2]

Moreover, numbers of people have devoted their energies, even their careers, to seeking destruction of the PC(USA), celebrating every defection from it. According to one search site's figures in late 2009, there were more than 3,192,000 references to "Presbyterian decline" and "Presbyterian demise." That represents more than one reference per member of our church! Some allege that the PC(USA) is "apostate," "a servant of the anti-Christ," and at the very least, "un-Christian." The diatribes, thank God, seem to have decreased somewhat in recent months, though detractors still publish invitations to schism in major newspapers and independent journals.

What has been happening in the PC(USA)—the loss in members, the vituperative critiques, and the proselytizing—has also occurred in the other mainline denominations. More recently, many more conservative American denominations, those commonly labeled evangelical Protestant churches, have also been losing members and receiving scathing criticism.

Further, and perhaps in part because of the negative publicity, younger Americans are less and less inclined to join any church in the first place—even those megachurches specifically focused on their age cohort. Increasing numbers of Americans today seek to be spiritual without "becoming religious" or joining a church. They relate negatively to the "binding" (from Latin *ligare,* meaning "bind, connect") in a community of any kind. This unwillingness to make commitments causes real concern.

But I am equally concerned about our diminished "presence" today and our future prospects as a part of the Christian movement and the body of Christ. Pundits today say American churches have in large measure "sold out," lost our zeal for the gospel, settled for a small "market share" of members' time, energy, imagination, and money.

The Presbyterian Church (U.S.A.), the portion of the Christian family in which we have particular responsibility, has been disproportionately significant since the founding of the nation. We have exercised a distinctive role in the spiritual and moral life of the nation. What will it mean for the other streams of Protestants if we Presbyterians have diminished zeal and influence? What happens to American life more generally?

Further, how can those of us seeking a vibrant future for the Presbyterian church and other constructive portions of the Christian church best contribute energy and resources?

Presbyterians in America

From the very beginning of the United States of America until today, Presbyterians have exercised a profound presence in the nation. Several American colonies, particularly the middle colonies from New Jersey to South Carolina, contained comparatively large numbers of Presbyterians. We were a major irritant in the face of the Anglican religious establishment and repressive colonial administrators almost everywhere.

Though early accounts of our history accented the leadership of Presbyterians in fomenting the American Revolution and carrying it to success, more recent histories show that some Presbyterians remained loyal to the British crown. So, numbers of us fought fiercely on both sides of that struggle, with many also seeking quietly to avoid the hostilities, just as we seem to have been on all sides subsequently in every major issue in American life.

Most Presbyterians emigrated from Scotland, Northern Ireland, and England. Significant numbers also came from Reformed communions in Wales, France, Holland, and several states that eventually comprised Germany and Switzerland. Each of these ethnic groups had been forced to make compromises in gaining or maintaining a Presbyterian presence with a state church. This was true especially for those Scots who had been exiled in Northern Ireland, the so-called "Scotch-Irish" Presbyterians, a large number including the only clergyman signing the Declaration of Independence—John Witherspoon.[3]

Presbyterians quickly came to gain African American and Native American members as well. Free persons of color, slaves, and those of mixed parentage became a significant part of colonial Presbyterianism. It took decades, though, for white Presbyterians to recognize formally the leaders from among the African American and Native American faithful, to educate them as pastors, and to ordain them as elders.

In several of the new states, Presbyterians could have lobbied to become a state church, as Congregationalists did in New England. But almost all of us wanted freedom of religion and disestablishment. As did the Methodists and the Baptists, the chastened Episcopalians, and dissenters from various European countries, we Presbyterians organized ourselves as a "denomination." We counted members who joined our congregations rather than including everyone within a geographical parish as part of the church, as European state churches had done until then.

In the new nation, our first Presbyterian General Assembly of 1789 authorized a delegation to greet newly inaugurated President George Washington and offer support. We arrived close behind the Methodists, who beat us there because their hierarchy moved with alacrity.

We Presbyterians were tottering as well as thriving in those early decades—at least in comparison with Methodists and Baptists. Both these streams of Protestants flourished in the new nation—the Methodists with good organization as their winning the race to Washington showed, the Baptists with their ability to divide into many congregations and seemingly have all of them viable. Both Baptists and Methodists considered formal theological education for pastors optional, though it was and still is a requirement for ordination in the Presbyterian church.

Presbyterians soon were far behind Methodists and Baptists in numbers of members, though we still grew despite our demand for a learned clergy and mutual accountability among pastors and elders. Our arrangement of comity with the Congregationalists (now the United Church of Christ) meant that few Presbyterian congregations existed in New England. Soon larger numbers of Catholics and Lutherans settled on the successive frontiers, so that Presbyterians usually numbered about fifth in numbers of adherents in most American regions.

We had already begun founding colleges in colonial times, and we increased that effort, along with the organizing of other institutions to support Reformed lifestyles—a strong movement for Sunday (termed a Christian *Sabbath*) observance; a vibrant Sunday school movement (first called *Sabbath school*) to evangelize children of unchurched families; and family religion, an expectation that families would engage daily in Bible reading and prayer together.

As public schools increased in number in the nineteenth century, Presbyterians cooperated with others in the major Protestant denominations, including the Lutherans in some areas and Christian Churches (later named Disciples of Christ) in others, to support them and help them flourish. Same with public libraries, free kindergartens, and hospitals.

We tottered as well with splits and some ethnically centered communions, with several Presbyterian denominations competing for members and influence. Presbyterians of every stripe invested heavily in both home missions and foreign missions. We sought to evangelize populations to the American West and in poor and segregated communities throughout the country, and we sent missionaries to many countries throughout the world, especially those in Africa and Asia.

This general pattern of a national Presbyterian presence continues to the present. We still have disproportionately large numbers of national leaders in politics, business, academic life, medicine, and in many other helping professions, but nowhere near the percentages from earlier decades.

Numbers of excellent books chronicle our history through the eighteenth and nineteenth centuries.[4] Several of them also lament lost opportunities for Presbyterian growth or predict the demise of Reformed Protestantism.

The *Presbyterian Presence* Study

In the 1980s, many of us became deeply concerned about these issues of declining membership and what we perceived as diminished zeal among Presbyterians. We also worried about what we termed a "theological malaise" among Presbyterians—a sense broadly expressed that we have in recent years succumbed more to culture wars and simplistic divides than we have attended to serious theological explorations of the gospel and its translation for our times. Thanks to major grants in the late 1980s from the Lilly Endowment, Inc., and the collaboration of scores of researchers, three of us led a massive study of the Presbyterian Church (U.S.A.) as a case study of American Protestantism in the twentieth century.[5]

Several of us assumed particular responsibility in the research project to explore in depth a reinvention of the Presbyterian church in the twentieth century to meet many new challenges—industrialization, urbanization, and the like. We discovered that indeed a "next Presbyterian church" had begun in the late 1800s, as in all the major denominations—more formal in organization and staff-driven, as opposed to its more informal and volunteer-driven predecessor. An incorporation of many Presbyterian congregations and councils at every level had paralleled the simultaneous incorporation of America in industry, commerce, and community life.

With the coming of the more formally organized congregations and denominations of the twentieth century, the church as a corporation replaced the looser confederation of congregations from the previous century.

Many of the characteristics of the PC(USA) we take as permanent actually are, at most, four generations old (some newer than that) and are a result of that incorporation. Consider professional staff in congregations. In 1900, few churches paid anyone other than the one pastor who served them, and that pastor usually farmed, taught school, or at least had a substantial family garden to supplement an inadequate pastoral salary. Directors of Christian education, music directors, choir leaders, pastoral counselors, support staff, youth pastors, sextons—all these professions and paid jobs arose in the twentieth century.

The organizational revolution in the United States that took place between 1875 and 1925 brought bureaucracy, professionalism, and complex economics to church life. Weekly offerings in worship services for operations and benevolences, church capital campaigns, mandatory pension payments, endowments, mortgages on sanctuaries, manse allowances, per capita assessments, special offerings—all arose in denominational life during this period. In the Presbyterian church it also brought increasing clericalism. As a result, there was increased dependence on pastors and other specialized ministers to speak for the church and to lead it at every level.

Strictly speaking, Presbyterians have no clergy. We ordain elders and deacons, as we understand the Bible teaches. Our new Form of Government, adopted in 2011, makes this distinctive Presbyterian mark very clear. But in the corporate model, teaching elders assumed the roles that priests and clergy exercise in other denominations. Our teaching elders are treated as clergy in the United States by both the military and the judicial system, and all of us use the term in general conversation. Presbyterian ruling elders—people who increasingly were board members in the burgeoning for-profit and nonprofit corporations in America—began functioning similarly for congregational leadership.

At the denominational level and in middle councils, the Presbyterians became more like a corporation as well. Our *Book of Order* began to expand exponentially, providing explicit rules for our worship, our calling of leaders, and our discipline.[6] An essay in our research project asked if the PC(USA) might be shifting again, this time resembling a federal regulatory agency, a body that places mandates on the membership, sometimes "unfunded mandates," yet not always providing resources with which to accomplish the required activities.[7]

Three Lessons among Many from the Study

Our most startling discovery confirmed among Presbyterians what other scholars were also beginning to assert at the time—that the Christian faith comes, humanly speaking, primarily from family life and from participation in a particular congregation. There are exceptions, to be certain, but most Presbyterians grew in faith deeply influenced by practices in their family of origin and in congregational life.

We identified a traditional Reformed ecology of formal and informal institutions that had characterized Presbyterian work and worship throughout the nineteenth and early twentieth century.[8]

The nature and force of what was termed *family religion* exercised great impact—father, mother, children, and others in the household regularly reading the Bible together, discussing the texts and their faith, and then praying together. This typical way of being Reformed Christians had been supported and encouraged by ruling elders and teaching elders who led family devotions in their own families and regularly examined families in their congregations, if possible. Presbyterian Sunday schools and Reformed Sabbath observance were the other two major institutions at the foundation of this Presbyterian ecology.

The exploration of this ecology, its thinning throughout the twentieth century, and questions regarding its strength today and its composition in the future are all crucial subjects when considering the future of the PC(USA).

A second important conclusion grew from our study of the ways Presbyterians are connected. We affirm that we began and continue as a connectional church, but we found that our church governing bodies, courts, or councils had changed the interpretation of what it means to be connected.[9] Further, we learned that most Presbyterians join, participate in, and depart from a local Presbyterian congregation, rather than thinking of themselves as joining, belonging to, or leaving the PC(USA) or its predecessor denominations.

At inception, and through the nineteenth century, presbyteries, synods, and the General Assembly "bubbled up" from the collaboration of congregations and, later, middle councils. So synods grew from presbyteries and the General Assembly grew from decisions made from less-inclusive councils. Their meetings and work were more informally organized than we had previously imagined.

Leadership varied depending on the situation and the personnel available. Together the congregations and their sessions gave money as they were inspired to do so for mission of various kinds. Church discipline was most frequently administered in congregations by sessions. Those who committed certain sins—drunkenness, infidelity in marriage, desecrating the Sabbath, and, occasionally, the mistreatment of slaves—received penalties, such as refusal of Communion.

Presbyteries saw to the ordination process, discipline, and sometimes expulsion of teaching elders. Synods oversaw institutions such as schools that served whole regions rather than just adjacent communities. And one today would describe the leadership as mostly bottom-up, predominant localism, and a confederation of congregations for the most part.

In the twentieth century, most direction and programming for the newly organized denominations was top-down, though representatives from congregations were responsible in presbyteries and representatives from presbyteries were responsible at General Assembly meetings. Gradually, staff from various offices in the councils formulated the frameworks for actions and frequently made executive decisions with the authority of the council. For several decades, through the first half of the twentieth century, this shift worked reasonably well. Presbyterians participated in "unified giving," and executives with their councils and committees determined the expenditures. In the United Presbyterian Church U.S.A, even the funding for synods came from allocations of unified giving funds by the General Assembly.

As in other institutions throughout America, unified giving in the PC(USA) diminished from its 1983 beginning. Presbyterians increasingly made designated gifts, in part to withhold from those causes with which they disagreed. In other ways, too, the connected nature of the Presbyterian church reverted to its previous, more informal and congregation-based practices.

We gained new insight concerning the way most Presbyterians view the Presbyterian church. To state the matter succinctly, most Presbyterians belong first and foremost to a local church, one in which families and individuals celebrate baptisms, weddings, and funerals. There they receive and provide pastoral care and Christian formation. People join that congregation because friends ask them to visit and come back, they like the preacher, the music, the services provided, the outreach accomplished, or all of these. They stay because they get involved; feel fulfilled in mind and spirit; and enjoy the fellowship, the mission, or other local ingredients. They leave because they move, sense less need for that community after a life passage, feel alienated, or believe the local culture has changed.

Only a small percentage of Presbyterians actually become involved in the wider denominational life of the Presbyterian Church

(U.S.A.)—its presbyteries, synods, General Assembly, seminaries, and other elements of its regional and national organization. Our two-church hypothesis pointed to a symbiotic relationship between the local church Presbyterians and the governing body Presbyterians.[10] In crass terms, the local church Presbyterians provide money, a pool of potential members, and the major "market" for the denominationally oriented Presbyterians, who in turn provide higher education and religious institutions, pastors and other professional staff, curricula, hymnals, expertise, and organization for the local church Presbyterians. In healthy times, the symbiosis works seamlessly, to the benefit of everyone. One can even see a shared piety and worldview—an obvious Presbyterian culture.

What we did not address to the same extent twenty years ago, nor could we foresee, was the current accelerated reconfiguration of American life and cultures, a restructuring that now augers quite a different Presbyterian future in the United States in years to come.

In the nineteenth century, and well into the twentieth, Presbyterians could readily identify particular Reformed doctrines and practices as their own. Observers from outside the church could characterize Presbyterianism as well. But can we still discern anything distinctive about our part of the Christian family? Is there an identity worth preserving for the future?

Study Questions

1. When you think of church, what comes to your mind first? Your local congregation? The Presbyterian Church (U.S.A.)? The "holy catholic Church" we affirm in the Apostles' Creed?
2. Is your church thriving? Tottering? Tinkering? How and why?
3. How did you come to believe in Jesus Christ? What people and institutions helped?
4. How do you and your church help others grow in Christian faith? Learn the Bible?

Chapter 2

Presbyterian Identity and Culture

*R*ather than simply listing again the traditional characteristics of Presbyterian theology and doctrine, let us consider a particular congregation at worship and at work. What can we learn of Presbyterian identity from examining its life? What of Presbyterian culture?

First Presbyterian, Burnsville, North Carolina: A Case Study

On a hill in the small county seat town of Burnsville, in the mountains of North Carolina, sits First Presbyterian Church. The church split twice in the 1990s, and elders say it was almost dead with fewer than twenty-five in Sunday worship. The session decided in 1999 to "go for broke," and they asked the Presbytery of Western North Carolina to match their resources to provide a full-time pastor for at least five years. They called Maggie Lauterer, a freshly minted seminary graduate from what is now Union Presbyterian Seminary in Richmond, and she came preaching and teaching, full of enthusiasm.

Pastor Lauterer and the session did not aim first at increasing membership so much as seeking to grow the capacity of the congregation to listen to and care for one another, develop in faith, and perhaps become more attractive for potential members by providing hospitality to whomever would come.

When on successive Sundays three young families, new to the town, came to visit in their church-shopping, she asked the session if they might host a dinner party. They invited these church visitors and included another potential member couple who also had children.

Pastor Lauterer, after a dinner prepared and served by the elders, invited the guests to describe the elements in a church that would be the "right church" for their family. Members of the session could hear for themselves what changes would make the church more attractive. Then she asked them to pray about their choices and ask God if they were being called to make that "right church" happen right here.

The session considered the stories, insights, opinions, and hopes of the young families. Over time, they sought to implement the ones consonant with Presbyterian worship and work.

All those folks became members, and some of them now, several years later, are strong leaders at Burnsville. Now, more families of all ages are joining and becoming quickly assimilated. People also come from areas around Burnsville. A number used to be members of Presbyterian churches elsewhere, but more came from other parts of the Christian family. A good number had been inactive for many years, and a few had no religious preference before they became part of First Presbyterian in Burnsville. Several former Quakers and a couple of former Mennonites have had profound influence on the sense of mission in the congregation and on its worship as well.

On the Sunday my wife, Carolyn, and I visited we found the worship service and the adult Bible study class packed. The church employed an open, welcoming theology, and the bulletin was crowded with opportunities for service and discipleship. Children led portions of the worship, and a middle-schooler, well-rehearsed and projecting his voice nicely for all to hear, served as liturgist. Pastor Lauterer and the children dramatically re-enacted the account of Moses in the bulrushes, replete with a one-year-old infant in a basket. The congregation repeated aloud the names of the midwives—Shiprah and Puah. The sermon included admonitions to be active in faith, as they were.

There was excellent music, with a great choir and superlative music director, an offertory violin duet by two teenaged girls, and robust congregational singing. Five new members joined that day—one of whom had been holding an infant through the worship service. Pastor Lauterer and ruling elders spoke afterward of mission trips; of care for the needy in Yancey County, one of the state's poorest; and of youth groups and mission partnerships with other churches in Africa and Latin America.

I just learned that Maggie Lauterer will soon retire, and First Presbyterian Burnsville will be looking for another minister. But members and officers in the congregation are confident and competent in offering their work and worship as praise to God.

Looking for What Is Presbyterian

When we examine the life of First Presbyterian Burnsville, or certainly most other Presbyterian churches, we find some distinctive marks identifying its Reformed witness to the Christian gospel:

- Note the shared leadership between elders and pastor—the naming mark for us. We took our name from the Bible, following both Old and New Testaments to find *elders* (from the Greek *presbyteroi*) called to lead God's people.
- Note the worship focused on Scripture in its complexity. We take authority first from the Bible and secondarily from confessions of faith that reflect implications of Scripture for God's people.
- Note the congregational singing and the offering of dignified music in worship. Yes, those who led the Reformation followed Scripture in that regard as well, and the singing of the Psalms still is characteristic of most Presbyterian congregations.
- Note the thoughtful approach to hospitality and the way the Burnsville session and pastor listen, assess, and then reform their practice as they balance the desires of the congregation and the possibilities within Reformed sensibilities.
- Note everyone is welcome at First Burnsville. Their life together is grounded in God's grace and our gratitude.
- Note that Presbyterians in Burnsville, North Carolina, are involved in God's mission both globally and locally. It does not exist to survive but rather to engage in witness and thereby attract others into its fellowship.

Most of these marks, and several more that we could note if space allowed, characterize almost every Presbyterian church in the PC(USA), whether the congregation is Korean American, self-consciously "evangelical," traditional in style of worship, predominantly African American, in a city, in the country, or anywhere else!

And since we consider sustainability for the future, it behooves us to examine what makes a church Presbyterian.

While all these marks are distinctively Presbyterian, none is uniquely so. Perhaps there existed at one time a uniquely Presbyterian recipe, a mixture of ingredients in proportions not found elsewhere in Christianity. But certainly in recent decades the variety in styles of worship and work among PC(USA) congregations is wide indeed. And a particular congregation's identity may resemble that of another congregation in the vicinity from another denomination more than it does the identities of Presbyterian congregations elsewhere.

When Reformers of the sixteenth century tried to cleanse the Western part of the Church, what we now call the Roman Catholic Church, some such as Martin Luther sought to keep as much as possible of the worship and governmental structure, following the Bible. Anglicans also sought church continuity with Rome as much as possible, while denying the power of the papacy. Others in the radical wing of the Reformation sought to jettison as much as possible the Medieval Church—doing away with ordination and sacraments and a sense of the one universal Church.

Ulrich Zwingli, Johann Hussgen (Oecolampadius), Heinrich Bullinger, John Calvin, John Knox, and a host of other men and women collaborated to balance continuity and change—to follow Scripture primarily. They did not scuttle traditions simply because Roman Catholics prized them, nor maintain those practices and theological tenets not found in Scripture. They sought a middle way.

Balance continues to characterize Reformed Christianity, in church life, in relationship to society, in bridging with human sciences and arts. It might begin with our holding on the one hand that "God alone is Lord of the conscience,"[1] while believing also that Christians stand a better chance of discerning God's will if we meet together in councils. Equally, it might originate from the belief that all of us are sinful except Jesus Christ, so we need to restrain the power of everybody.

We even seek a balance in attention to the persons of the Trinity. Believing strongly in the sovereignty of God, we also affirm the sole authority of Jesus Christ. At our best we also attend equally to the power of the Holy Spirit.

Reformed theologian Karl Barth pictured the preacher holding the Bible in one hand and the daily paper in the other, balancing the verities of Scripture with contemporary insights and applications. Presbyterians who translate Scripture into various languages also speak of the balance between keeping the original meanings and interpreting the Bible so people can understand the Gospel of Jesus Christ today. Presbyterians who attend to our historic Westminster Standards and the other confessions of faith we profess know of the balance between following those confessions and following Scripture itself.

All those characteristics of our life together share respect for *words*. We Presbyterians are people of the Word, seeking to follow God's Word and Jesus Christ through words about him in Scripture, through preaching, and through confessions of faith.

Presbyterians and Confessions of Faith

We in the PC(USA) adopt confessions of faith; we are a confessional church. While members make a profession of faith and a session examines them "in the meaning and responsibilities of membership" (*Book of Order*, G-5.1303) they are not required to believe according to our confessions. Our elders, however, both teaching and ruling, affirm in an ordination vow to "receive and adopt the essential tenets of the Reformed faith as expressed in the confessions of our church as authentic and reliable expositions of what Scripture leads us to believe and do" (*Book of Order*, W-4.4003c). Elders are asked, "Will you be instructed and led by those confessions as you lead the people of God?" (*Book of Order*, W-4.4003c).[2] If a congregation elects deacons as well, those officers make similar promises.

The confessions affirm the sovereignty of God; the sinfulness of human beings; the atoning life, death, and resurrection of Jesus Christ; the quickening power of the Holy Spirit; the nature of the one universal Church as the body of Christ; the power of God's grace to redeem those who profess Jesus Christ; and the promise of eternal life. Some of our confessions also speak of other essential tenets, such as relationships among people, the reconciling love of God that Christians can reflect in living, and the nature of our sacraments—baptism and Communion.

What makes an essential tenet for all Presbyterians? How do Presbyterian essential tenets in confessions relate to our affirmation that Jesus Christ alone is Lord of the conscience? We have struggled with these questions since the very beginnings of American Presbyterian churches.

Presbyterian Parties

Wise historians have discerned that Presbyterians from England, Puritans especially, considered the Bible and patterns of Christian practice as essentials. These proclivities led them to zeal for the gospel—ardor in faith. Scot Presbyterians, including the Scotch-Irish, relied more heavily on the Westminster Standards and frequently sought subscription to the Westminster Confession of Faith and the Westminster catechisms. Presbyterians with other ethnic origins brought their different understandings of the relationship of Bible and confessions, practice and belief. They focused on discipline and organization of the church—order in Christian life.

Ardor and order.

Splits and unions occurring among Presbyterian communions from colonial times to the present have been thoroughly explored and explained—sometimes accurately but frequently in partisan broadsides and angry diatribes. For the present task, considering our sustainable future as the PC(USA), it suffices to say there exist today several types of Presbyterians.

Most analysts (and partisans) in recent years have simply said some of us are conservative and some are liberal. Most simply, conservative Presbyterians are said to center more on Calvinist orthodoxy as found in the Westminster Standards and on the saving work of God for individual Christians. Many have come to use the term *evangelicals* amid the wider use of that term in American Protestantism.

Liberal Presbyterians are said to center on corporate Christian life, in the church and in the wider world. The Christian gospel is seen as essentially more social in nature, and witness has included social witness to the powers and principalities.

In recent decades the Presbyterians for Renewal and the group of organizations that make up the Presbyterian Coalition have represented a conservative, evangelical side of our PC(USA), and the Witherspoon Society and the Covenant Network of congregations and individuals have represented the liberal or progressive side. Presbyterians in the Renewal or Coalition party opposed ordination of practicing homosexual ministers and elders, for example, regardless of whether they remained committed to one partner or not. Members of the Covenant Network sought to require the same discipline and accountability among homosexual ministers and elders as among heterosexual ones. The fact that the PC(USA) in 2011 ceased to bar men and women from ordination just because of their sexual identity as practicing homosexuals produces increased anxiety that the denomination will not survive.

At the time of our study of the Presbyterian presence twenty years ago, and from others at the time, it seemed that the PC(USA) included three parties, with one liberal extreme comprising 10–15 percent, one evangelical extreme with 20–25 percent, and with most Presbyterians in a middle position. The left wing generally supported ordination of gays and a woman's right to choose concerning abortion. The right wing vigorously opposed both. Both sides cited biblical warrants for their positions, though neither homosexual behavior nor abortion procedures as presently practiced are treated in Scripture.

The majority middle party, it seemed, could see both sides of both "hot-button" issues. On abortion, the middle party generally considered there should be fewer, that abortion was sinful, and that the government should not forbid it. On ordination of practicing homosexuals, members of the majority middle party found biblical warrants compelling and contradictory, and they frequently made comparisons to the ways Presbyterians have reversed stances on other social issues—slavery, divorce, and the role of women in church leadership. This majority middle party also considered Presbyterian essential tenets to include both individual piety (or spirituality, as it had come to be called) and responsible social witness as both mission and evangelism. By this understanding of Presbyterian parties, increasing understanding and tolerance of gays and lesbians among those in the middle resulted in the recent change in church policy.

Successive Presbyterian panels show that since 1993 larger percentages of Presbyterians have come to identify themselves as "very conservative" or "conservative" (34% in 2008). At the same time, the percentage of people who identify themselves as "liberal" or "very liberal" has also grown (25% in 2008). Still, almost half the members of the PC(USA) (41%) are self-proclaimed "moderates."[3]

The insight of Jack Haberer bears the ring of truth—that Presbyterians belong in one or more of five distinct "GodViews." In his book *GodViews: The Convictions That Drive Us and Divide Us,* Haberer asserts that from our varied theological and cultural backgrounds as well as from our differing psychological dispositions, we prize special aspects of the Reformed faith. Some of us are *confessionalists,* with a passion for the truth of the gospel. Others of us are *devotionalists,* thirsty for spiritual refreshment. Still others of us are *ecclesiasts,* paying special heed to the church itself and its health. A fourth part of us are *altruists,* seeking to live the gospel in service to others, especially the poor. And finally, a fifth part the PC(USA) today is primarily *activists,* overcoming injustice in the world.

Haberer shows at length how all five are based in Scripture and how all are important for the whole denomination. His book invites Presbyterians to enjoy differences in identity within the PC(USA), to learn from one another and pray for one another rather than seeking to excise a differing party or perspective.

Such a perspective on our identity within the large tent of the PC(USA) seems more applicable than those employing the metaphors of right and left, conservative and liberal—facile labels that derive from our political life. Identifying five parties within our one denomination also keeps us from thinking only yes or no to a given issue. Social analysts such as Deborah Tannen say that by reducing complex issues to binary ones we create an "argument culture" especially through mass media and the point-counterpoint method of presenting social issues.[4]

The reference to culture produces yet another question about the PC(USA): Do we have a common culture? We can talk easily about our identity. We know we possess an identity. Many of us think we can express its essence. Our culture, on the other hand, is more subtle, present in our life together whether we realize it or not. Formal and informal institutions work together among us implicitly and sometimes tacitly to give us similar perspectives and shared meaning in life.[5]

Is There a Presbyterian Culture?

With the conclusion of our *Presbyterian Presence* study, I became part of a team led by Jackson Carroll and Wade Clark Roof, which studied the decline in denominationalism. My research question: "Is there a distinctive Presbyterian culture?" I read extensively, listened to others on the team speak of denominational cultures, and interviewed denominational executives at the time, asking if they discerned one. If so, how did it affect their work?[6] Since that time in the 1990s, I have remained attentive to the findings, and the marks of a Presbyterian culture remain discernible, perhaps even more pronounced today.

Almost every Presbyterian leader said, "Yes. There is a special Presbyterian culture." They named eight marks.

- We pay close attention to the "Word of God"
- We are wordy in our educated, literate discourse and writing
- We value order, and our orderly form of government
- We relate faith to ordinary life, balance personal and corporate faith
- We sit uneasily with ostentatious displays of wealth
- We bear elitist tendencies, if we are not downright participants in elitism
- We seek to be inclusive in our worship and ministries
- Our culture consists primarily in mission

In each case, those interviewed used the word *word* in telling of the distinctive culture of Presbyterianism. *Word* prizes both our faith and the Scriptures, while it points us to Jesus Christ. All Reformed Christians pay attention to the Word. Listen to Reformed Christians and you will hear: "We are all people of the Word—Jesus Christ." Those I interviewed told of Christian symbols and stories that meant so much in times of crisis. Their conversations were highlighted with allusions to Bible stories and church history.

One spoke of the compassion she received and the well-phrased letters of support even from those in the congregation who disagreed with her when she was subpoenaed on a government matter related to the sanctuary movement: "In composing my response, I discovered just how Presbyterian I am—depending on the Bible and church teachings." She laughed as she pointed to someone with a T-shirt that read "Presbyterians do it decently and in order."[7]

Another denominational leader named the fact that we find authority in the Old Testament as well as the New Testament. He also perceived that our historic dependence on the Psalms and the prophets led us into distinctive hymnodies and ethical stances that now are more commonplace in Christianity broadly. In 1993, he spoke of our need to listen more to God's mission for us.

Presbyterians, disproportionately from the teaching professions, with more than our share of lawyers and librarians, also value literate sermons, substantial Bible study, and care in spelling and grammar. These proclivities probably stem both from our respect for words, our wordiness, and our elitist tendencies. An African American Presbyterian leader told me he observed that American racial and ethnic minority congregations are usually more insistent on these marks of our culture than are some predominantly "white" congregations, "that tend to get sloppy and take such things for granted." Another African American director said she observed that "if a board or committee member at denomination headquarters speaks in poor grammar, the moderator will frequently repeat the statement in correct phraseology."[8]

Even in the mid-1990s, Presbyterian leaders expressed worries that our Presbyterian culture would soon disappear. The complexity of granting authority to both Old and New Testaments, of honoring education and the worship of God with our mind, of literate and respectful discourse, of considering blatant displays of wealth unseemly, of seeing Christianity as God's missionary enterprise—all of these marks of Presbyterian culture seemed imperiled.

Nobody sought to maintain a Presbyterian church as a brand, seeking more members as a kind of market share in American religion. Those interviewed then, and everyone in shared conversations presently, seek the preservation of these Christian marks at least as leaven in the loaf of worldwide Christianity. Most would prefer for these marks to prevail among Christians more generally. Certainly, many Presbyterian and Reformed communities throughout the world maintain these cultural characteristics. But can they be sustained in the United States? Can Presbyterians viably embody them in the future here?

Yes, by the mercy of God it seems there is a sustainable future for the PC(USA). We now depend on a new ecology for faith development. We enjoy a new way of being connected, or rather we have seized again the former ways we enjoyed denominational connections. And we can share rich resources from Presbyterian institutions and elsewhere to support a faithful presence in the future.

Study Questions

1. What marks are most important in confirming your Presbyterian identity? Shared leadership? Biblical authority? Congregational singing and participation in leadership of worship? Hospitality for all? Mission?
2. What similarities and differences do you notice between Presbyterian work and worship at First Presbyterian, Burnsville, and that in your congregation?
3. How do you conceive of the different "parties" within the PC(USA)?
4. How does your congregation study the Bible? The PC(USA) confessions?

Chapter 3

A New Presbyterian Ecology

A new ecology already helps form the worldview of and influences the faith of Presbyterians. In sociological terms, the effectiveness of our part of the Christian family is and will be determined in large measure by the vivacity of that ecology. To speak theologically, the Holy Spirit quickens faith and guides the process of faith development especially through the influence of formal and informal institutions in the life of a believer. As St. Paul used the illustration of parts of a body working together, so the many formal and informal institutions cooperate. That mysterious process of growing into Christ Jesus is God's work, and we know only that we can foster that holy work as we exercise discipleship and seek God's will in our lives— individually and together with others.

The Traditional Presbyterian Ecology

When we studied the Presbyterian Church (U.S.A.) some years ago as a case study in mainstream Protestantism in America, we found new elements that did not seem to fit in the Presbyterian ecosystem for faith formation.[1] As we all know, an ecology consists in the variety of flora and fauna that mutually provide life for each variety of organism participating in it. The trees, plants, wildlife, and even the bacteria live off one another and nourish the whole system. On a seashore you will find two, three, or maybe even four ecosystems side by side—one among the plants and animals on the beach itself, one next to it in the tide pools and brackish marshes, and yet another in

22

the coniferous or mixed forests a few hundred yards inshore. If there are abutting cliffs or mountains, yet a fourth can be located at some height from sea level.

The traditional Presbyterian ecology from the founding of the new nation came to consist in a symbiosis among many formal and informal institutions. At the core of that ecology, according to thoughtful leaders at the beginning of the twentieth century, were three major ingredients—family devotions, Sunday schools, and Sabbath observance. Surrounding and supporting those three central institutions were numbers of others, which we on the Presbyterian Presence research team explored in some detail—Presbyterian orphanages and schools, Presbyterian hospitals, Presbyterian colleges, Presbyterian seminaries, Presbyterian presses, Presbyterian retirement homes, and even Presbyterian cemeteries.

Missionary endeavors also played a significant part in the traditional Presbyterian ecology. The term *missionary society* as a description of the Presbyterian denomination became a watchword, first of the so-called old school as Presbyterians suffered a split in the 1830s and then of all the major Presbyterian denominations in post-Civil War America. They supported domestic missions, planting new congregations on the successive western American frontiers and organizing churches among racial and ethnic minorities and in blue-collar neighborhoods in their own locales. And they provided people and money for foreign missions especially in many areas of Africa, Asia, and South America.

Presbyterians organized women's circles and auxiliaries mainly to support missions. They held revivals and special services. Weekly prayer meetings and collections from the Sunday schools focused on specific missions and programs. And Presbyterians received inspiration and enthusiasm for ordinary work and work from the stories and accounts provided by returning missionaries, especially of the sacrifices made by newly converted Christians and leaders in indigenous churches.

The situation was more complex, of course, than just a parochial Presbyterian ecology feeding, self-reflexively, the faith development of Presbyterians. Many of the institutions in the traditional ecology were shared with other Protestant strains also predominant in many parts of the nation—Methodists, Congregationalists, Baptists,

Disciples of Christ, Lutherans, and Episcopalians. Sabbath observance, for example, depended on legal inhibitions from ordinary
commerce and recreation. Blue laws were passed to forbid commerce, mail delivery, use of public spaces for sport activities, even
sometimes the restrictions on public thoroughfares. And each of the
other Protestant traditions offered distinctive parochial institutions
for faith development of members.

These mainstream Protestant cultures shared informal dominance
of the public schools as they developed, and frequently also generated the founding of land-grant colleges and public universities. The
armed forces chose chaplains exclusively from these traditions. With
increasing urbanization, metropolitan cemeteries were opened for
Protestants to share, while Catholic and Jewish cemeteries existed
apart.

We found many of the elements in that Presbyterian ecology, so
vibrant throughout the nineteenth century, had withered or perished
in the twentieth century. A distinct minority of Presbyterian families
now gathered regularly for Bible reading and family prayers. Sabbath
observance among Presbyterians had almost entirely disappeared
by the 1960s. The once raucous, evangelizing, and lay-led Sunday
schools that thrived, teaching Bible and Presbyterian catechisms in
congregations and reaching out to poor children and racial minority
populations in cities, had been domesticated in the twentieth century
to become "church schools," an educational arm of the congregation
led by trained Christian educators if at all possible. In most congregations, the church school had decreased in size and scope to serve
only children of the congregation and perhaps some adults.

We did locate some new elements in the ecology, as we then
termed the innovative programs—Heifer Project International,
Young Life, United Ministries in Higher Education, World Vision,
Habitat for Humanity, and more.[2] These new institutions, however,
did not seem to foster Presbyterian faith development directly, and
sometimes they seemed even to draw Christian energy away from
Presbyterian affiliation and nurture. In many Presbyterian churches
such activities were not viewed as part of the life of the congregation, just an activity of a member or of several who were interested.
The projects and institutions were seldom mentioned in worship or
church school classes.

The New Presbyterian Ecology

Now, twenty years after discerning that an ecology had produced a Presbyterian-type practice, after discovering how the vibrant institutions of yesteryear have fallen into disrepair and sometimes disappeared, and after locating some that could be supportive of growth, we find that these and other innovative programs and charities have come to play a significant part in faith development. Many of the new ingredients in mission and faith development are now baptized in the worship and educational efforts of Presbyterian congregations. They no longer seem out of place or competitors for Presbyterian growth and witness. A tipping point has been reached and passed. We are now in the midst of a new ecology, not just replacing some dysfunctional and disappearing elements in the traditional one. The new ecology may incorporate some elements from the old one, to be sure, but the new ecology bears little resemblance to the previous one.

Most Presbyterians report they pray regularly. In many households, Presbyterians still pray together. And according to studies of our religiosity, most of us read the Bible and consider it God's authoritative word for our faith and life. A good number of us participate in Christian education classes, and some congregations still have vibrant Sunday schools. But the Christian Sabbath, a Sunday with no commerce and work, is almost extinct. And the seamless movement from one to another Presbyterian institution is seldom in our experience. Rather, we draw intentionally on the elements in the new ecology to fashion a coherent whole amid a whirl of competing possibilities.

Again, the traditional ecology has not disappeared. It simply does not exercise the same power for faith development as it once did. Presbyterian hospital systems still exist, for example, in New York City; Charlotte, North Carolina; Albuquerque, New Mexico; and elsewhere. But they do not rely on members of the PC(USA) for staff, volunteers, or governance any more than on the rest of society. People still grow up Presbyterian, but most adult members of the PC(USA) have come from other parts of the Christian family, from other religions, or from secular life.

To begin making the case for a new Presbyterian ecology, consider five essential characteristics of it:

- it is ecumenical
- it construes the Christian family inclusively
- it defines Presbyterian work and worship in fluid terms
- it employs digital technology and social media more than printed and published literature
- institutions and practices bubble up from the interests and passions of members rather than being received from people in authority. In the same vein, Presbyterian leadership itself bubbles up rather than being gained from external authentication from participating in successive parochial institutions.

We will consider some other possible characteristics in chapter 10. But for now, let me explain the first five characteristics briefly. Then we can examine some cases to see the differences at ground level.

The new ecology is ecumenical. Where previously the Presbyterian ecology shared many elements and institutions, the center of its character lay in its distinctive Reformed and particular core. Presbyterians grew up in families where the parents belonged to Presbyterian churches. Presbyterians were noted for their learned clergy and restrained worship practices, exercised in almost all Presbyterian institutions. Even in its raucous early years, Presbyterian Sunday schools were generally more restrained than those of other parts of the Christian family. Presbyterian leaders—deacons, elders, and ministers especially—came mostly from Presbyterian families. Presbyterians went to public or Presbyterian-parochial secondary schools and graduated from Presbyterian colleges. And if they became pastors, they attended Presbyterian seminaries as well. The marks of distinctive Presbyterianism, when compared with most other similar denominational life, included love of study and literate discourse, frugality in lifestyle, and a love of the Bible (and other books). Presbyterians were typically labeled "bluestocking," and their demeanor led outsiders to mark them as "God's Frozen Chosen."

Presbyterians were typically ecumenical to a point within the Protestant hegemony. They looked to include representatives from other parts of Protestantism when they sought to fill positions on the boards of Presbyterian colleges, for example, and they collaborated with Methodists, Baptists, and Congregationalists to pass blue laws restricting business on Sundays. Some single-issue associations for public education, rights of working people, prison reform, and other voluntary societies began with Presbyterians and extended throughout evangelical Protestantism. Likewise, Presbyterians and their councils frequently endorsed single-issue initiatives from elsewhere.

But Presbyterians took pride in being born and reared in the faith of their fathers. The Scotch-Irish especially maintained an ethnic hegemony in much of the interpretation of Presbyterian history, especially in areas such as Western Pennsylvania and the Carolina Piedmont. If a practice seemed foreign in origin (foot washing, for example, which was practiced in the radical Reformation traditions, or high liturgy in worship, which to some seemed Catholic), Presbyterians eschewed it. John Calvin, John Knox, and whichever Anglo-American preachers were in vogue constituted the major sources of biblical interpretation and homiletical fashion.

The new ecology is ecumenical at its core, rather than on its edges. A majority of Presbyterians, in fact, come from other portions of the Christian family, from other religions, or from that rapidly growing portion of American society which is labeled by demographers NRP (no religious preference). Biblical scholars employ the insights of Roman Catholic and Eastern Orthodox interpreters as rapidly as those of Reformed thinkers. Congregational practices come from Mennonites as quickly as from Methodists, and students of congregational practice declare that greater differences in worship and work exist within the Presbyterian church than between Presbyterians and those of other persuasions in the same region or culture.

The new ecology construes Christian family inclusively. Previously among Presbyterians a stable family consisted for the most part of a husband, a wife, and children. Presbyterians built Sunday school curricula on such a model, even after World War II when a wider variety in types of families had become more common in the American demography. Family devotions, graded curricula for children, the use of volunteer parents as ideal teachers, the expectations of youth fellowships for parental support, and many other parts of Presbyterian life reflected such a construal.

Much has been made in recent years of the Ozzie and Harriet stereotype during the 1950s and 1960s, when so many family patterns had already changed in light of rising numbers of divorces, two-parent wage earners with no children, same sex couples, and single-parent families. Were Presbyterian families becoming as diverse in composition as the rest of the society during those post-WWII years? Since so many of the Presbyterians were middle class, might the two-parent, traditional family have remained typical among Presbyterians longer than among society in general?

Whatever the history of the changing family, it is without doubt that Presbyterian congregations now overwhelmingly construe the nature of the family as inclusive. Family night dinners and church school classes are constructed expecting the heterogeneous forms of families to predominate. Blended families, single-parent families, and "grandfamilies" (grandparent(s) with grandchildren) light the Advent candles for congregational worship without explanation or apology. Intergenerational camps and mission trips have mostly replaced the family camps of yore (which still may be termed Family Camp but welcome all types of families).

The new ecology draws on a whirl of work and worship together. The original ecology was built on the assumption that Presbyterians would experience the interdependent institutions in a linear fashion—a young person growing up in a Presbyterian family, for example, attended a Presbyterian youth group while in college, joined a Presbyterian church subsequently in the neighborhood where the new family lived. The adult church school class could assume this grounding in previous instruction, and the selection of elders and deacons for congregational leadership could assume knowledge of Presbyterian polity from an apprenticeship in it. Pastors and Christian educators came from an extension of that ecology, attending Presbyterian seminaries or schools for Christian education. At least that model predominated.

Today, as we well know, the ecology for Presbyterian growth and faith development assumes very little about other institutions that might have contributed to someone's possessing knowledge of Presbyterian identity and culture. So many members of Presbyterian churches also attend other churches for worship, fellowship, service, and instruction. We normally explain our worship in the bulletin, and our educational efforts usually assume no prior knowledge of the subject (an irritation to some born and reared Presbyterians).

Sociologist Wade Clark Roof, quoting Walter Lippman who quoted Aristophanes, terms the current situation: "Whirl is King, Having Driven Out Zeus."[3] He recites the bewildering mélange of activities and sources of spirituality available in our society today. He argues these influences frequently are at odds with one another, seldom with an arbiter to judge among them for quality, consistency, and coherence. He asserts that we now cobble our religious and spiritual worlds in a process of reflexive spirituality.[4] Coherent worldviews in such a whirl of activities and competing authorities are difficult to attain, demanding an intentional weaving of work and worship to make a single, spiritually sustainable fabric.

Another sociologist, Robert Wuthnow, describes the process as continually "tinkering." He claims that younger people particularly are "tinkerers," pure and simple. They put together a life from whatever skills, ideas, and resources they find at hand. They delay marriage, make patch-quilt careers with multiple jobs, and live contentedly with looser relationships.[5]

We will return to explore this mark of our current situation as we plumb ways to address the future and seek a coherent Presbyterian ecology for years to come.

The new ecology relies on digital technology and social media. Where we have seen Presbyterians as both people of the Word and also wordy, we have also, in the traditional ecology, honored books and periodicals, bought them, read them, received authority from them. We still rely on books, but the new ecology expands the kinds and scope of words and images.

The great majority of Presbyterian churches now maintain a Web site to communicate with members and to attract prospective members. Even small congregations frequently attend carefully to their digital "face" on the Web, exhibiting their mission statements, calendars, profiles of staff, and photos for all to see. Most Web sites provide directions to the location of the church building, and some even offer profiles of members and invitations to make contact online or to visit the church.

Facebook and Twitter are constant tools for Presbyterian pastors seeking contact and maintaining pastoral relationships with young people. Jim Kitchens, who serves the Calvary Presbyterian Church in San Francisco, remembers having joined Facebook reluctantly in a previous Nashville pastorate and now considers it a primary tool of pastoral care. "People in San Francisco use PDA's and text. Period. It's indispensable for me."

Finally, the direction for a Presbyterian congregation bubbles up, primarily, from the interests and passions of the members of that church and its leaders, including those of the pastor. Mission projects, faith development efforts, theological perspectives, levels and goals for financial support, and emphases in worship vary enormously among congregations.

Frequently such contextual focus is intentional. "Money follows members of White Memorial in mission!" is the succinct phrasing of this characteristic for one church in Raleigh. This was a frequent saying of Art Ross, who served as pastor until recently, and is now a virtual mantra for budgeting. The Presbytery of the James, in Virginia, has adopted a pattern of supporting interest groups, needing only a few people to begin a project or petition for support.

But even where local bubbling up is not recognized as the determining factor for projects and perspectives, congregations recognize its import when alerted. Nancy Ammerman, sociologist and analyst of congregations for decades, explains that few Protestants today receive traditions or denominational authority. Rather, Presbyterians are building networks of faith; communities for fellowship; and even traditions for worship, faith development, and Christian education. She asks, "Does denominational citizenship still exist?" and answers the question affirmatively. But she emphasizes the activity of participants in the church as more important for mainstream Protestants than any denominational imprimatur or the words of national or regional officers.[6] Permit an illustration from recent experience to illustrate the new ecology and its dimensions outlined here.

Williamsburg Presbyterian Church: A Case Study

Saturday afternoon. After a prayer together, a busy scene of whirling activity unfolds. Despite apparent confusion we are carefully organized—a hundred and more of us. Some of us are seated at tables—measuring rice, dried vegetables, and vitamins and placing portions in plastic bags. Each packet will hold sufficient ingredients for six people to receive a nourishing meal when hot water is added.

Others of us are sealing the packages. Still others of us run the sealed packages to tables where eager packers place them in boxes. Finally, another bunch of us takes the boxes to load them in the truck. Four-year-olds, grandmothers, cub scouts, members of the Canterbury Club (the college group from nearby Bruton Parish Episcopal Church), friends from First Baptist Church (a predominantly black congregation across the street), the youth group from St. Bede Roman Catholic Church, elders, deacons, families, members of a high school soccer team—all working together to pack meals for people in Haiti.

Oh, and each time we have packed a thousand meals, a kid is chosen to ring the big gong. A resounding "GONG!" reverberates in the room, and we all applaud. Soon we have packed 40,000 meals. Gifts from various individuals and congregations—about $11,400 in all—make this project possible. And the nonprofit group Stop Hunger Now, well-experienced in bringing together resources to accomplish this project and then distributing the meals in places of need, affords such opportunities for service on almost a daily basis in our region at various churches.

"What is that on your T-shirt?" one adult asks a member of a youth group, whose shirt says simply: "8:32."

"I don't know," the young man replies.

"It's John 8:32," a nearby boy responds. "Jesus said, 'You shall know the truth, and the truth shall make you free.'"

"Mommie, why are we doing this?" one little girl inquires.

"Jesus told us to." The mother quotes Matthew 25:35, in a voice loud enough for the whole table to hear her. "'I was hungry and you gave me something to eat' He said those people would be welcome in heaven."

As we leave, having vacuumed up the leftover rice and other remains, one of the prim octogenarians says with a smile, "This is what the church is supposed to be!"

In Sunday worship, the next day, the pastor brags on the number of meals we put together for shipment abroad in the course of inviting people to be good stewards of God's gifts.

The New Ecology at Work

Here is a typical engagement of Presbyterians today. The initiative bubbles up from two ruling elders and some members of the congregation who heard of it from members of another church. The money comes from members of the congregation as special giving—not an item in the budget. The opportunity is communicated on the congregational newsletter online and the social media employed by some young people.

An executive for Stop Hunger Now, who formerly served as a pastor before finding vocation in this nonprofit, brings volunteers from across Tidewater, Virginia, and the equipment and commodities for the endeavor. Presbyterians "host" the event, but we do not count who belongs to what faith as people stream in to help. We trust the packages of food will be faithfully distributed among the Haitians in need, for we have heard through various sources that the stewardship is effective.

We can note briefly several of the characteristics of the new ecology for Presbyterian faith development if we follow the experience closely. Note many people of differing groups and denominations are working together on a common task—feeding the hungry, something Jesus told disciples to do. Catholics, Baptists, and doubtless others are invited, participating and helping underwrite the costs of the effort. It is ecumenical at its core.

The old and young find space for one another at the table. Afterward several of the older participants speak appreciatively of the chance to work alongside the children. Everyone can do something together.

And to one looking on, the scene is quite confusing. Overheard conversations meld to make an aural cacophony, a swirl of fluid relationships and a mix of instructions, greetings, farewells, and expressions of meaning. The gong sounds, and to an outsider it seems disconcerting. To the participants, however, the resounding noise symbolizes achievement. The swirl has meaning, and informal instruction for discipleship occurs with the use of T-shirt designs that provoke questions and teachable moments for children.

A church event for Stop Hunger Now may epitomize life in the new ecology, but it scarcely touches its complexity and pervasiveness. To explore that ecology, we can examine some activities and experiences of other congregations and communities.

Study Questions

1. What parts of the traditional Presbyterian ecology affect you in your growth in faith? Sunday school? Sabbath observance? Family devotions? Other elements?
2. How do you see the new Presbyterian ecology at work in your congregation? Ecumenical involvement? Inclusive understanding of "family"? The fluid relationships between work and worship? Reliance on new technology? Leadership bubbling up from members?
3. How does your congregation make decisions about work and worship?
4. In what ways does your church practice hospitality? Use digital technology effectively?

Chapter 4

Institutions and Elements Comprising the New Ecology

*M*any institutions and elements comprise an ecology for faith development. We have already identified five significant characteristics of the new ecology for Presbyterians, and we can study how they work together. But in trying to analyze their effects, we need to remain modest. There may be many more elements than we can recognize at first inspection.

Some of the most influential elements in the traditional ecology were so pervasive and subtle that most Presbyterians took them for granted. Having regular family times for reading the Bible and praying together, for example, was just what Presbyterians did—not something they analyzed. In the same way, most just thought Sundays were for worship and family, not a time to do regular business. In the same fashion, I imagine some of the most pervasive and influential ingredients in the new ecology we cannot yet discern and identify as helping us grow in faith.

Examination of some congregations can teach us more about the roles of the five identified characteristics in our new ecology. Perhaps this examination will suggest the presence of other elements as well.

First Presbyterian Church, Binghamton, New York:
A Case Study

For six years, First Presbyterian Church of Binghamton, New York, has sponsored Ronaldo Baptiste who lives on the Island of St. Vincent in the Caribbean. Each month they give money to ChildFund

International to supplement the meager wages of Ronaldo's father, a day laborer. Children in the congregation regularly undertake projects that raise money for Ronaldo's education and medical care.[1]

The ChildFund sponsorship of Ronaldo Baptiste is just a portion of the ministry of care offered to those in need by First Presbyterian, Binghamton. The congregation also supports a YWCA shelter care program for women; Meals on Wheels; a food pantry; Interfaith Builders; a Samaritan Counseling Service for families; and other local, regional, and international service programs. In some of the efforts people donate time and in-kind gifts. In other cases they give money. Different portions of the congregation pray regularly for all their mission efforts to be successful in meeting human need. In all cases they collaborate with other churches and social service organizations. The list of benevolences changes from year to year, but some in which people are particularly invested remain constant.

You might be tempted to see First Presbyterian, Binghamton, as a declining church, with fewer than half the members it once had. But the Presbyterians there now are anything but dispirited. Their smaller numbers simply mean everyone must do everything possible. No one has the luxury of being a spectator.

The church building, located in a depopulated neighborhood of needy people in the heart of the city, is appropriately situated to provide dinners every Tuesday night for anyone, regardless of need. Other churches help them, including members of West Presbyterian Church, which has voted to merge soon with First.

Christ Presbyterian Church, Edina, Minnesota: A Case Study

Christ Presbyterian Church (CPC) is a newer and larger congregation in a still-growing, more affluent area of the Minnesota Twin Cities. This church of more than five thousand members is explicitly evangelical in its worship and work. Its evangelism and mission are interlaced thoroughly, and its Statement of Faith includes the Apostles' Creed, speaks of the uniqueness of Jesus Christ, and the primacy of Scripture "inspired by God and authoritative to direct the behavior of God's people in matters of faith and practice."[2]

CPC invites members and friends to join a special partnership with World Vision, sponsoring children in Moyo, Zambia. They call it "Growing Hope." "The rural community of Moyo struggles with inadequate health care and limited educational opportunities," according to the CPC Web site.[3] "Sponsoring a child is a way to make a tangible impact on this community as we help them reach self-sufficiency." By paying $35 per month, a member can take special responsibility for a child, and the whole family will benefit from the support as well.

"In Moyo," according to Paul Tshihamba, Pastor of Missions at CPC, "11% of the children die before they reach the age of five. Of the estimated 30,000 people there, 50% of the households have orphans and vulnerable children."[4]

The partnership for serving in Zambia grew from a previous relationship with a WorldVision project in Uganda. Over a fifteen-year period, members of CPC had sponsored as many as 1,500 children at a time there, bringing support for development of the whole community. As that community reached self-sufficiency, leaders from CPC and WorldVision sought another appropriate location for partnership.

Paul Tshihamba and others from CPC were impressed with the indigenous leadership for the project in Moyo, so they began to go in mission trips there and to encourage support from fellow members of CPC. "We are biased in favor of indigenous leadership wherever we serve," Tshihamba explains. "Perhaps because I came from the Congolese Presbyterian Church originally, people are even more ready than usual to hear about the importance of growing young churches as we engage in mission and evangelism together."

The partnership for Moyo is paired with yet another Christian community in Zambia. There, pastors and other church leaders receive education to become change agents for local Christians and their communities. In Goma, in the Ituri District Republic of Congo, yet another similar partnership with CPC is under way. These efforts, and a score more of local and global partnerships—the International Justice Mission; an international human rights agency working to free those in slavery, sexual exploitation, and other forms of oppression; Questscope, working in low-income communities in the Middle East to transform the lives of at-risk youth and women; and more. Some partnerships are more explicitly evangelical than others, though certainly not more Christian than the Moyo Project. The feeding of the hungry, clothing of the naked, and providing clean water for the thirsty are, as Jesus states in Matthew's Gospel, equivalent to caring for the Messiah himself.

"We structure our overall mission with a commission of sixteen leaders, eight focusing locally and eight focusing globally," Tshihamba explains. "Then each ministry is supported by a task force coordinated by these leaders. More than 100 of us travel each year to the mission partnerships locations." Another pastor, Mike Holz, takes special responsibility for the local engagement of CPC. A missions administrator, Leslie Boie, with support staff and interns, round out the paid leadership devoted to missions. But everyone at CPC emphasizes how all the ministers—paid and volunteer—share responsibility for leadership and support one another in worship and work.

Assessing ChildFund, World Vision, and Other Similar Charities

The active ministry of Monica Styron, pastor at First Presbyterian, and the involvement of elders and other leaders in the congregation partake thoroughly of the new Presbyterian ecology. Note the ecumenical, pluralistic, and inclusive institutions in which the people of First Presbyterian invest—ChildFund, Meals on Wheels, Interfaith Builders, Samaritan Counseling, YWCA, and others. Note they are merging with another Presbyterian Church, combining resources and reimagining a future based on the new challenges they hear God calling them to meet. Note that involvement in each of these missions and benevolences bubbled up from the particular interests and context of First Presbyterian, Binghamton.

The multifaceted and complex mission and evangelism outreach of CPC in Edina equally participates in the new ecology—perhaps even more profoundly than First, Binghamton. The partnership with WorldVision, for example, is systemic in nature, not just incidental. From CPC's initiative, WorldVision helped select an appropriate project, one that offered indigenous leadership meeting the criteria of the CPC pastor and lay leaders. The work is with all kinds of families—vulnerable children and AIDS victims especially. CPC supports Middle East as well as African projects in Muslim regions as well as Christian areas, seeking to develop Christian leaders there. And out of the cobbling of partnerships comes a coherent identity for CPC, as expressed in the Statement of Faith it constructed.

In the traditional ecology, Presbyterian congregations gave primarily to Presbyterian programs for mission and benevolence—presbytery, synod, and General Assembly level programs both nationally and in partner Reformed churches in other lands. Susquehanna Valley Presbytery, where First Binghamton belongs, and Twin Cities Presbytery, in which Christ Presbytery participates, both offer mission and benevolence programs and projects. The congregations participate in those Presbytery projects they choose and they pick whatever other efforts they wish.

Likewise the Presbyterian Hunger Program, Self-Development of People, and other denominational efforts continue to offer channels for giving and participate in mission and service. In the previous ecology, Presbyterians in these congregations would likely have thought first of the Presbyterian channels. Many congregations still do. But today almost all Presbyterian congregations are drawing heavily on the resources and reach of major nonprofit charities. The nonprofit charities not part of denominations have enormous appeal, special emphases, first-rate marketing, and quality controls that are visible and publicly accessible. Moreover, most of the major charities have deep Presbyterian involvement.

At least 260 Presbyterian churches sponsor children through Child-Fund, for example. Thousands of individual Presbyterians sponsor children and support projects. In fact, the charity was founded in 1938 by Dr. J. Calvitt Clark, a Presbyterian minister who had been a missionary in China. Clark knew firsthand of the suffering of Chinese children. He had seen the devastation. So he started a China Children's Fund, based on the sponsorship (first termed *adoption*) of individual orphans by individual Americans. In collaboration first with Methodists and then Baptists, Episcopalians, and Catholics, he led China Children's Fund to become the Christian Children's Fund, as the charity expanded to support orphans and other poor children in several countries. Today it is ChildFund International, with affiliates in thirteen other countries forming The ChildFund Alliance, providing $300,000,000 a year for poor children and their families and communities in thirty-eight countries.

Although Presbyterian involvement in ChildFund has been significant through the years, the charity has never been part of the traditional Presbyterian ecology. World Vision International, the largest of the American-based sponsorship charities, has roots more in nondenominational Protestantism. But Presbyterians have been supporting its efforts from the very beginning of the organization. Stan Mooneyham, World Vision President from 1969 until 1982, was Minister-at-Large for the Palm Desert Community Presbyterian Church. Rich Stearns, the current president, is at University Presbyterian Church, Seattle. Bob Steiple, president from 1987 until 1998, also came from that congregation. Roberta Hestenes, a Presbyterian minister, served almost a decade as chair of its board of directors and as its international pastor-at-large. Leighton Ford, Stephen Hayner, John Crosby, and John Huffman are just a few of the Presbyterians who have recently served on the board of either World Vision International or World Vision, USA.

The American Institute of Philanthropy, which rates charities according to transparency, stewardship of resources (spending less than 25% of revenues for administration), and other criteria, gives "A" ratings to both ChildFund and World Vision. Other major sponsorship charities such as Compassion International, Save the Children, and the Christian Foundation for Children and Aging, each with Presbyterian involvement, also receive top marks.

Other Major Charities in the Ecology

The Habitat Ministry Team of Myers Park Presbyterian Church in Charlotte, North Carolina, has built a house every year for more than two decades, and it helps coordinate and staff Habitat projects in El Salvador.

Hundreds of other congregations—large, middle-sized, and small—build houses with Habitat for Humanity. Twenty years ago, when we began exploring what we then called "new elements in the ecology for Presbyterian faith development,"[5] we found most of the Presbyterian Habitat groups were not closely integrated into the rest of the life of the church. The situation now is quite different. Worship at many churches includes the commissioning of volunteers periodically, regular prayers for them in worship, and reports of their work on Web sites and newsletters for the congregation. Many congregations include line items for Habitat in their annual budgets, and most others figure the out-of-pocket expenses as part of their benevolences.

Heifer Project International is yet another strong component in the new ecology. It has a structural relationship with the Presbyterians, for one of its five Covenant Agency directors usually comes from the membership of the Presbyterian Hunger Program Committee of the PC(USA). Eight denominations, including the Methodists, Episcopalians, Lutherans, Disciples, United Church of Christ, and Roman Catholics, all share in naming directors, along with the Church of the Brethren, which was the denomination of the founder, Dan West.

These major charities not only engage in serving the needy with food, health care, educational opportunities, and community development, but they are also deeply involved in helping the American governmental agencies dispense food, clothing, and shelter. Equally, their experts work with United Nations agencies and those of many countries in setting policy and providing models for self-development in poor, emerging nations.

Ten Thousand Benevolences

Ten Thousand Villages is yet another charity with which many Presbyterian congregations are involved. It, and others like it, support indigenous craftspeople and makers of other useful and artistic items in many countries throughout the world, frequently in partnership with Presbyterian and other churches there.

Ten Thousand Villages began in 1946 as a Mennonite businesswoman sold fair trade items first from the back of her car and then at festival sales in churches. The Mennonite Central Committee adopted the program in 1962. With several name changes over the years, the effort grew to become worldwide, ecumenical, and economically self-sufficient.

But the suggestive number is helpful in describing the myriad efforts of Presbyterian congregations, some unique to one location, and many more regional, fluid networks of volunteers. Jeff Ryan, pastor of the College Park Presbyterian Church in Orlando, Florida, tells of Operation Christmas Child, in which members of the church give, collect, and package small presents for needy children around the world. The small, rather new congregation he serves welcomed families from the neighborhood, hospitality that led to the sense of family extending more broadly. Pastor Ryan believes the recent recession led the members of College Park to be more concerned for the poor. So now they have begun to serve as a relay facility and are known within the community as a place of generosity and caring.[6]

First Presbyterian Church in Grand Forks, North Dakota, supports Heifer International and Kids in Need, a part of World Vision, but the church also supports the Northlands Rescue Mission, a ministry with homeless and mentally ill people in twenty-one counties surrounding Grand Forks. Trinity Presbyterian Church in Chinle, Arizona, ministers to the Toyei assisted-living program for severely mentally ill in the Navajo Nation. They also have a place, Ama Doo Alchini Bighan, for abused women and family emergency use. That church, in turn, received support from a sister Trinity, Trinity Presbyterian Church, of Palm Coast, Florida.

As you might imagine, the benevolences of Presbyterian congregations are many and varied. They are also multiplied by the projects and programs of sister congregations in other parts of the world. In similar fashion, the educational endeavors of Presbyterian congregations today are many and varied. Some are evident in the case studies already discussed—Interfaith Builders and Samaritan Counseling Centers, for example, which serve spiritual development within the congregation at First, Binghamton as well as for those outside. Space limitations permit only a glimpse at several more.

Members of First Presbyterian, Binghamton, would probably consider themselves on the liberal side of Presbyterianism, if they stopped to think about it. Members of Christ Presbyterian, Edina, would doubtless say they are conservatives for the most part, certainly on the evangelical wing of the PC(USA). But both are remarkably similar in their embrace of the new ecology. Equally, other congregations studied rely on the new ecology regardless of their place in the denominational spectrum. In fact, as I quizzed leaders of some of the conservative and liberal issue-oriented organizations in the PC(USA), they uniformly acknowledged that they collaborate with similar affinity groups ecumenically, that they assume an inclusive understanding of family; that they employ digital technology and social media extensively; that they depend on leadership bubbling up from rank and file; and that they must continually tinker in order to locate a coherent, Christian stance on the issues on which they focus.

Spiritual Development in the New Presbyterian Ecology

Outreach feeds "in-reach," so to speak. More properly, the pursuit of God's mission for First, Binghamton, and Christ Presbyterian, Edina, feeds life together in the church. So the Christian formation and spiritual development in a congregation is one with the pursuit of God's mission. Is that what Jesus meant by saying those who lose their lives find them, individually and corporately?

Achieving a coherent community with worship, faith development, fellowship, and mission means "regular practice that requires discipline and study,"[7] according to Carol Howard Merritt, a pastor at Western Presbyterian Church in Washington DC. She also points out that we cannot predict how God's presence leads us. "Forming spiritual communities is like painting," she explains. An artist practices and engages in the disciplines, loses herself in the work; "but then suddenly something begins to move inside her. She picks up the brush, after some time she feels stirred internally and externally, and creates a work of great beauty."[8]

The Bend Youth Collective meets weekly in Bend, Oregon, summoning youth from the Presbyterian, Lutheran, and Episcopalian churches in town. Their motto is, "3 Churches—1 Community, 3 Traditions—1 Faith, 3 Histories—1 Future." Greg Bolt, Associate Pastor at First Presbyterian, and two colleagues from the partner congregations lead what they call "the radical step." "We seek to serve our community with energy, passion, thought and whole lot of fun—together," they claim.[9]

The Ginter Park Presbyterian Church in Richmond, Virginia, has for a number of years offered a twenty-four-month-long program for youth based on an Episcopal Church curriculum called "Journey into Adulthood." Each group of students engages in an ecumenical, interfaith pilgrimage. The recent one to Borderlands Education and

Spiritual Center in the Black Hills of South Dakota involved both study of Lakota spirituality and Benedictine disciplines.

Since it began in 1990 in the Presbyterian Church of Barrington, Illinois, the Workshop Rotation method for Sunday school has caught on in hundreds of congregations across the country—churches of many denominations and theological flavors. The pastor of Barrington Presbyterian, Neil MacQueen, and its educator, Melissa Hansche, claimed they experimented with it first because it solved problems, such as the lack of preparation of teachers and the lack of biblical literacy among those who attend church today. They focused on major stories from the Bible, and over time many creative leaders joined in to offer resources. Students rotate among workshops for which leaders can prepare well, repeating their "lessons" in interactive ways with new groups each Sunday. It also fits nicely for children from blended and other, newer types of family situations who may not be able to attend every Sunday, for each session is somewhat self-contained. You can tune in easily through a free Web site, where churches swap ideas and offer resources for one another: www.rotation.org.

These programs and resources only begin to describe how elements of the new ecology feed local congregational life. We shall find some more in succeeding chapters as we examine the worship and work in additional Presbyterian congregations. So many different charities and partnerships would seem to dilute Presbyterian identity and culture. Mysteriously, this does not prove the case in many Presbyterian churches. How can a church maintain and perhaps even enhance its Reformed identity while drawing on such a variety of possibilities?

Study Questions

1. Compare the outreach of your congregation with that of First Presbyterian, Binghamton, and Christ Presbyterian, Edina. What similarities and differences can you observe?
2. What other elements in a new ecology can you discern in addition to those already named?
3. How does your church focus on spiritual formation and Christian education for new Presbyterians?

Chapter 5

Integrity and Agency in Presbyterian Worship and Work

*I*f whirl has become king, if we are cobbling new ways of being Presbyterian, then how can we maintain that identity and culture that has distinguished Presbyterian life? John Buchanan, Moderator of the 208th General Assembly, keeps reminding Presbyterians that our Reformed tradition has always been and remains a "living tradition" that "resists being pinned down too precisely."[1] It is not easy, says Buchanan, for Presbyterians today to maintain what he calls "good faith."

But we can see it done in hundreds of congregations across the denomination. Take the King's Grant Presbyterian Church, for example.

King's Grant Presbyterian Church: A Case Study

At the King's Grant Presbyterian Church in Virginia Beach, you can sense almost immediately that the church has it together. Whether you go for the early worship, with a praise band and more informal worship style, or you attend the more traditional service at eleven o'clock, you will be greeted by smiling folk welcoming you warmly. The church mixes church school curricula as it mixes styles of worship. Young families and older adults greet one another and introduce visitors during the passing of the peace, which can extend for five minutes or more as everyone circulates throughout the sanctuary—even the children and youth.

The leaders of the congregation come from among those who have belonged for decades and those who recently joined King's Grant. Some will speak with you about their service in Kairos, an evangelical ministry in prisons, and others will describe their participation in interfaith ministries.

The pastor, Sel Harris, explains that King's Grant Presbyterian Church takes seriously the ordination of elders—not just for their terms of active service on the session but even more for their continued leadership afterward. "After three years of active service, the elders really know our mission and our life together. It's in that fourth year, rotating from session, that numbers of them sense calls to take on new responsibilities. And they do great in the work! They call themselves 'The College of Elders,' and they meet periodically to plan and to consider new ministries for the congregation and new callings for each elder."

Pastor Harris names Julie Seipel as one example of this calling of veteran elders. Julie Seipel serves as the volunteer staff person for youth ministry. She says she loves the work and undertook it because the church needed a stronger ministry not just for young people in the congregation but for others as well. The young people take mission trips and study together regularly. Now she's moving from leadership of the senior highs to help rejuvenate a junior high group.

Julie Seipel speaks of her service as a vocation. "It makes sense for me to serve this way with my children growing up in this church as well as working with others. We all serve as teams—four of us for the high school kids and now five more for the junior highs. Several of us are elders, and a couple of us are back on the session now." She attends staff meetings at the church as she is able, and she goes to conferences and continuing education events as well. She is more knowledgeable about the church and youth ministry than many who have received degrees in that area of ministry.

Julie Seipel, Sel Harris, and others in the youth group leadership team took fifteen of the young people to Mexico on mission trips for several years in a row. In 2011, however, they went to El Paso to work with the border ministry churches there. "Flying and driving with the kids is as much fun as the work itself, and we all get to worship together, sometimes with those we are meeting on the trip."

When the earthquake hit Haiti, Julie Seipel and other leaders in the congregation immediately organized a massive effort to provide emergency food for the victims. They arranged for Stop Hunger Now to come to King's Grant two weeks later. They raised money to provide for 250,000 meals to be packaged and sent immediately to Haiti.

Sel names ruling elder John Morison as yet another of these elders called to particular ministries at King's Grant. Morison, a retired executive from public television, is leading a group of eight elders in thinking about what he terms "the next big idea for King's Grant." After listing a number of ministries and innovations he asks the group to listen to experts concerning the church and the community, to pray together and plan, and to summon a report to present to the next meeting of the College of Elders. Out of that series of meetings and discussions comes a report, provided for consideration by the College of Elders, then presented to the congregation. It envisions ways to restructure leadership, seeks suggestions for providing more thorough hospitality, and asks about future staffing needs.

Adapting and Thriving in the New Ecology

At the King's Grant church, the session carefully assesses its program and mission. They actively adapt within the new ecology in the Presbyterian way—with attention to Scripture, lots of prayer, extensive readings in various areas that inform church life, and meetings of some duration. They listen broadly and think to include people in the congregation, those not yet in the congregation who might be attracted and even those of other religious traditions. City planners, leaders from other congregations, the presbytery executive—all receive a willing ear.

This careful and continuous process of planning and evaluation, the bookends for every mission effort and worship service, permit leaders at King's Grant to discern appropriate ways to worship, to help one another grow in faith, to enjoy fellowship together, and to serve those in need. They are constantly tinkering to make their work and worship appropriate, attractive for others, meaningful for participants, and faithful to the Gospel of Jesus Christ.

Many analysts of congregations claim we need to transform our Christian life for a future in which we will be sustained or perish. In fact, as the King's Grant leaders know, we need to adapt to an ecology in which we are currently being sustained. Adaptive leadership occurs within the already-changed environment of work and worship.

Just as the image of a church as an organism living in an ecology comes from the field of biology, so does the image of adaptation. In biological terms successful adaptation "has three characteristics: (1) it preserves the DNA essential for the species' continued survival; (2) it discards (reregulates and rearranges) the DNA that no longer serve the species' current needs; and, (3) it creates DNA arrangements that give the species' the ability to flourish in new ways and in more challenging environments."[2]

This definition of adaptive behavior might seem reasonable and straightforward. But it is extremely difficult work. To effect adaptation in Presbyterian churches where people grew up in the ecology that once proved effectual, with certain ways of worship and patterns of congregating, agents must convince enough people to hang in there with the changes occurring. The pull of the past can be formidable even when everyone can perceive how different the current situation has become from that which gave meaning and effectiveness in other decades and generations. So it is crucial to locate thriving Presbyterian congregations, ones that preserve essential marks of Presbyterian identity and culture, discard those practices that are today dysfunctional, and create new arrangements that permit congregations to flourish.

Many Presbyterian churches thrive today. These congregations, in other words, translate the Gospel of Jesus Christ again for yet another Christian era of faithful presence as Christ's body. In the field of biology, thriving organisms reproduce successfully. In churches, thriving also involves reproduction—increasing the measure of meaning and joy in praise to God among members of the congregation and being attractive so others can join in work and worship. How do you know if a church is thriving? Ask the members and leaders, and also ask those in the community who are not members of it.

King's Grant Presbyterian Church is thriving, as are the other Presbyterian churches highlighted in case studies thus far. The same applies at numbers of other PC(USA) congregations. Third Presbyterian Church in Richmond, Virginia, now offers five worship services each week. Pastoral staff, liturgists, and others who took part in leadership the previous week meet with those who will lead worship the following to assess what has taken place and to plan what will soon happen.[3]

At White Memorial Presbyterian Church in Raleigh, North Carolina, staff meetings regularly include the reading together of the bulletin and the newsletters that will be duplicated for worship and information among the congregants. They do correct misspelling and grammar sometimes. Remember they are Presbyterian! But more than that, they coordinate planning through the calendar and mentally rehearse the liturgy for worship.

The adaptation and creative ways of forging a coherent, Reformed life in a congregation is variously labeled "traditioning" and "fluid re-traditioning." Works by Nancy Ammerman and Diana Butler Bass explain the process for mainline churches.[4] As we saw in chapter 3, the new ecology has replaced one that was in many respects "given" for the local congregation. Now in each context, Presbyterian congregations that thrive are fashioning a way of being that is their own.

Such successful adaptation takes leadership and care, continuous practice, good thinking, and compassionate care from pastors and elders. It also takes some courage and wisdom, prayerfully attained, to support congregations as adaptation to the new ecology takes place. This adaptive leadership might best be termed *agency*.

Imagination + Follow Through = Agency

Sel Harris, Julie Seipel, John Morison, many members of the session and the College of Elders, and some who teach and lead worship at King's Grant are able to imagine constructive ministries and worship experiences. These ministries are helpful for the congregants and those in the Tidewaters area of Virginia Beach and Norfolk, and sometimes even for people in other parts of the world. One big reason these programs are so effective is that this group of people is able to work together.

Some analysts of American culture now term this ability, *agency.* "Agency is a generative force that inevitably leads to the matter of call," according to Gary Gunderson. "It gives traction to three questions: 'What am I to do with my life?' 'What have I been called to do?' and 'Am I doing it?' "[5]

Agency consists in a willingness to experiment and to act in creative ways. But it also consists of being disciplined and staying on task, as teachers term the mature actions of learners. It requires self-confidence and humility at the same time. In colloquial terms, it consists in "get up and go" while resisting a temptation to "go off in all directions at the same time."

"As agents, humans are self-determining beings who are in charge of their own conduct," says Richard Morrill, who considers agency the first characteristic of leadership. In speaking of Christian agency, we can say more explicitly that a sense of vocation and an ability to listen for God's word underlie agency as leadership. It takes agency to engage in adaptive leadership.[6]

Adaptive leadership, according to Ronald Heifetz and colleagues, is "the practice of mobilizing people to tackle tough challenges and thrive."[7] Heifetz advises those leading adaptive change to "get on the balcony" from time to time, to consider the whole of the challenge and the ways to meet it. We can all get caught up in the dance on the dance floor, according to Heifetz. We see our partner and those immediately surrounding us, but on the balcony, we can observe the entire event.

Again, adaptive leadership, according to this point of view, takes multiple participants. One person cannot accomplish it alone. The leader(s) optimally "regulate the anxiety" of the participants, providing tension sufficient for action but not so much as to overwhelm the people engaged. Heifetz repeats the adage, "Give the work to the people."[8]

The agency and adaptive leadership exercised by Presbyterians are patently evident at many thriving Presbyterian congregations. The qualities are apparent especially among elders and others in a turnaround church such as First Presbyterian, Burnsville.

After I told a group of Presbyterians about Burnsville, a friend directed me to the *Presbyterian Outlook* article on the Caldwell

Memorial Presbyterian in Charlotte, North Carolina. There, a dwindling congregation tottered on extinction and decided to close their doors. But as Charles McDonald, the interim pastor, made the announcement, a young couple asked if they could still join. They brought friends from a house church group, several of the couples interracial and some gay and lesbian. Soon the numbers in worship had multiplied, and they were able to call John Cleghorn, a second-career pastor straight from seminary. Numbers of people exercised agency, and they met adaptive challenges with creativity. Now ministry centers on Caldwell Memorial's homeless shelter for women, its ministry for Latino families, and outreach to spiritual seekers in the Charlotte area. Cleghorn, a thoughtful and experienced agent, credits many for the miracle, including the senior saints, those older members of the church before its turnaround.[9]

Others told me of the Elmwood Presbyterian Church, a three-site congregation with worship and work in East Orange, West Orange, and Newark, New Jersey, the largest predominantly African American church in the PC(USA). Members and presbytery colleagues credit Pastor Robert Burkins, called there in 1987, for creative and adaptive leadership as the membership has tripled and ministry has multiplied. Pastor Burkins in turn credits scores of youth leaders, choir and worship leaders, and those who take responsibility for Harambee Ministries to "help strengthen and build nurturing families in East Orange, NJ and the surrounding communities."[10] Since opening in 1994, the initiative has educated more than 1,500 preschoolers, preparing both African Americans and Latinos for successful educational experiences, and 200 young people have learned about technology and media construction for the entertainment industry.

For years, Clifton Kirkpatrick has been telling Presbyterians in positions of responsibility that we need many leaders to step up and work together. When he served as the Stated Clerk of the General Assembly for twelve years at the turn of the twenty-first century, Kirkpatrick frequently contrasted the Presbyterian style of previous generations (a few high-profile leaders in each denomination) with the current situation in which distributive leadership prevails. "So now we need more people, and each of us needs to do constructive work. If we can, our contribution as a part of the whole church will be strong and faithful."

Fostering Presbyterian Integrity and Agency

In the less regulated, more fluid atmosphere our new Form of Government affords, Presbyterian integrity and agency should flourish. In the words of Jill Hudson, who relates denominational offices with those in presbyteries and synods, sessions of congregations and other councils need to be "permission giving" for ministry. She says it does not mean giving up accountability, but it does mean giving up some control. "Empowering members to be leaders means freeing them to do the ministry to which they feel called—without waiting nine months for seven layers of approval!"[11]

After all, we now can draw on the gifts, skills, experience, and interests of both men and women, of young and old, of every color and background. Some PC(USA) leaders are suggesting that we think in terms of higher commitments that some are making: immersion educational experiences for ruling elders and other leaders, and networks across the denomination.

Jack Haberer suggests that we learn from the Roman Catholic "parallel universe" model of dual allegiances. Many leaders are members of religious institutes and orders, and all recognize the authority of bishops, cardinals, and the pope. A central hierarchy shares authority with parallel religious communities. Catholics have an hierarchical pyramid, and those called to missions, teaching, healing, and other such pursuits also can be part of the Benedictines, the Jesuits, the Sisters of Mercy, or the Dominicans—a host of religious communities throughout the world.

Haberer suggests that while Presbyterians surely do not want bishops and popes, we do have church councils—presbyteries, synods, and the General Assembly. And we also have networks, affinity groups, and other communities that claim our loyalty. In his view we could do well to recognize and encourage these parallel allegiances, share in the leadership, and share the work generously. Of course, there are more challenges than any of us can accomplish.[12]

A sustainable future will involve Presbyterians in imaginative new structures and will call for all the resources that congregations can summon. Officers and members of Presbyterian congregations can look within their own ranks for untapped resources and can learn from one another many best practices for the future.

Study Questions

1. Compare the work and worship of the King's Grant Presbyterian Church with your own experience of Presbyterian congregational life. What similarities and differences do you find?
2. In your experience who exercises agency well in your congregation?
3. What adaptive challenges face your congregation today? How can you meet them with agency and integrity?

Chapter 6

Presbyterian Congregational Resources

*I*n the mid-1970s my family belonged to Harvey Browne Presbyterian Church in Louisville, Kentucky, a predominantly white city congregation of several hundred members. We were impressed already with the large number of deeply committed elders, deacons, and church school teachers, as well as the pastoral leaders in that congregation. But as white segregationists in Louisville provoked a crisis by resisting the court-ordered bussing of students, scores of resourceful people at that church worked for reconciliation and constructive public education.

Naturally, the church was replete with teachers, principals, librarians, counselors, and others who possessed broad knowledge of the educational system. These were men and women of goodwill who cared about the community. They sought to move us all toward a more just society. They, and others from businesses and professions, brought to the situation competence in organizing meetings and strength in supporting one another. Harvey Browne leaders joined with leaders from other congregations black and white (sadly, there were few integrated churches in Louisville at that time) to host round after round of get acquainted times, prayer meetings, and forums.

We loved seeing people who seldom came to worship now join in, alongside those who led the worship and work regularly. Congregational resources were deeper and broader than we could have imagined before the events. The months of meetings and dialogues brought a measure of sanity and optimism to the public arena, and doubtless lessened the threats of violence as well. One of the pastors, reflecting some time later on the resources of the Harvey Browne members and officers, remarked that "This church had lots more going for it than I thought we had."

It is true that many congregations do not have the resources of a church like Harvey Browne Presbyterian. Nor do all public issues come as sharply defined as "school bussing," with its rabble-rousing opponents threatening riots. But on the other hand I am convinced that Presbyterian congregations typically have lots more going for them than they think. Perceiving the opportunities for ministry, eliciting the congregational resources, and drawing on a large group of leaders are all significant elements in a sustainable Presbyterian future.

Let's glimpse a slice of life at C. N. Jenkins Memorial Presbyterian to look further at the issue of congregational resources.

C. N. Jenkins Memorial Presbyterian Church, Charlotte, North Carolina: A Case Study

"Become a Friend of Freedom School" invites readers of the Sunday bulletin at C. N. Jenkins Memorial Presbyterian Church to make a contribution to support at-risk students by volunteering and by giving money for the program. The bulletin also recites the mission of the congregation: "Recruit, Respond, Revive, Rejoice." Audiovisual technicians, pastors, greeters, ushers, and ruling elders all collaborate in preparing for each of the three worship services every Sunday. Pamela Nelson directs the choir and Ron Monroe is minister of music as the congregation sings exuberantly. Saxophone, bass, drums, and piano usually constitute the instrumental ensemble, but organ and other instruments are frequently backing up the men's choir, the youth choir, or the young adult choir as they perform anthems.

Freedom School is just one of a score of mission efforts in which the congregation participates and contributes leadership. The pastors, Jerry L. Cannon and Eustacia Moffett Marshall, are deeply involved in interfaith ministries, ecumenical organizations, African American church groups, and ministerial bodies as well. Many leaders at C. N. Jenkins have high-profile positions in banks and other businesses in the Charlotte metropolitan area. Other leaders are people of modest means and hardscrabble backgrounds. "What makes C. N. Jenkins such a great place to worship and work," explains Pastor Cannon, "is the ability of the folks here to 'check profiles' at the door. We unite arm in arm and hand in hand with one accord toward the benefit of all."

Technology at C. N. Jenkins is first rate, and it has been for years. In 2004, C. N. Jenkins hired its first communications director, Julie Rudisell. She works with pastors, staff, and ministry teams to ensure consistency in communications. Donna Singletary, who confesses that she has a hearing impairment, credits the accessible AV as the "icing on the cake" there, leading her to deeper participation in worship and now to receiving a call to ministry herself. A visit to worship at C. N. Jenkins shows good acoustics, articulate lay liturgists, superb preaching, excellent music from choirs and instrumentalists, warm fellowship, and a vibrant educational program.

Trustee Eric McCaw, who serves as superintendent of the Sunday school, says the Web presentations and good digital hospitality serve to draw people into the congregation. But he credits the social ministry of the pastors as the primary means of evangelism. He thinks the extensive use of social media and the good Web site authenticate the appeal of C. N. Jenkins to newcomers. "Both the IT team and the AV team here are first rate," he explains. McCaw should know, since he is a network manager for a computer company.

Elder Jason Haskins, also in IT professionally, says the e-mail, Facebook, and other electronic communications from the church help him in his leadership ministry and preparing for worship as well. "C. N. Jenkins is an accepting, loving, family-like congregation for my family and me, and the use of technology only enhances our experience there," he testifies.

The Wealth of Resources in a Congregation

Whether the congregation is Harvey Browne in Louisville, or C. N. Jenkins in Charlotte, or another of those congregations studied thus far, leaders perceive ways of locating and employing the resources of the members. In fact, the remarkable wealth of skills and interests, experience and talent among Presbyterians continues to amaze those of us who study congregations. The challenge for most congregations is to employ more of the resources already present among members, deacons, and elders.

The Freedom School Partners program, another organic part of the new Presbyterian ecology in the Charlotte area and elsewhere, originated with the Children's Defense Fund, a Washington DC-based nonprofit. But several Charlotte-area Presbyterian churches, including Seigle Avenue Presbyterian and Selwyn Avenue Presbyterian are also involved, along with Baptist and Methodist congregations. They sponsor sites and offer summer tutoring and literacy instruction in a supportive setting with adult volunteers—lots of them. The churches also contribute funds to underwrite the six-week-long program. C. N. Jenkins contributes lots of human and financial resources to this ministry.

The pastors and session of the C. N. Jenkins Church give careful attention to technology in support of the Freedom School and dozens of other ministries and programs. They ask people with the skills and experience to lead a variety of "ministries" related to congregational work and worship—all the way from acolytes to an HIV/ AIDS awareness program. But note some of those with knowledge of technology choose to lead in other ministries, with the blessing of all the leaders. Eric McCaw, for example, enjoys serving as a Sunday school superintendent. But with his profession as a network manager, he offers reserve resources in IT and AV while content to let others serve there.

Additionally, each of the members who spoke about the work and worship of C. N. Jenkins told both of hospitality within the church and public witness outside it. Leaders there are exercising resources both for pastoral care among members and evangelism in the wider world. Again, pastor Jerry Cannon hesitated at my mentioning the fact that the church welcomes executives and working people alike. He worried that it might call attention to differences in social status among members. But he was willing to have the words included because it might help other churches become more inclusive.

C. N. Jenkins, and Harvey Browne too, make use of the skills and experience of a larger percent of the members than do some congregations, although some smaller congregations, such as First Presbyterian, Burnsville, seem to use the talents of almost everyone.

In a study helpful for churches of every description, Scott Thumma and Warren Bird claim that in most congregations, as elsewhere in society, 20 percent of the members engage in most of the ministry—and do most of the work. They advocate ways to engage the other 80 percent, first through a disciplined time of listening, then development of learning teams, and finally through leading efforts that draw on the strengths of members and aim everyone toward spiritual development.[1]

C. N. Jenkins involves as many as possible in the multiple ministries of the church. Its health, in part, stems from the expectation that there are no spectators among its members. I have found such a broad expectation of ministry in other thriving congregations as well.

At Highland Presbyterian Church in Louisville, a growing urban congregation, no fewer than seven church-wide systems exist to provide pastoral care for members, ensuring that everyone receives appropriate attention and prayers. Elder George Rau explained that everyone "kind of expected" to be with other Highland members at home and work, in small groups and elsewhere. Pastors visit in homes, a rarity now in many urban congregations. But they go chiefly where Stephen Ministers, trained volunteers working one-on-one with the homebound and those in nursing homes, tell them to go. Christmas Tree Ministry assures that everyone in the church receives attention at holiday time. Ruling elders visit members, especially making certain the Lord's Supper is provided for them regularly. Deacons have responsibilities for visiting and caring as well. Scores of members are involved in refugee ministries, another area of pastoral care that results in some new citizens joining Highland. And still others are regularly providing rides to church for older members who can no longer drive.

At the Bayside Presbyterian Church in Virginia Beach, several ministries focus on stewardship while they engage in service and evangelism, and three retired accountants share the duties of church treasurer. Worship teams in that congregation also work in the Minutes for Mission program that explains weekly how financial resources are allocated and what the congregation has accomplished with generous giving.

These few examples illustrate a special portion of the work of a Presbyterian congregation. Such churches are giving careful attention to worship, fellowship, teaching, witnessing, mission, and pastoral care—the major ingredients in Presbyterian congregational life.

Today, as in the past, Presbyterian congregations are relying on the resources of other congregations as well as on the talents of their own members. We have viewed the anticipated merger of smaller congregations in Binghamton, New York, selling whichever property could be most attractive to others while consolidating their efforts in worship and work. But some such small congregations have for decades shared pastors and found a special identity as a parish.

Since the 1940s, several rural and county seat Presbyterian churches in Southern Indiana have worked together in an informal parish arrangement. Appalachian congregations in Kentucky and West Virginia have done the same. The Pioneer Parish of Northern Waters Presbytery involves five Presbyterian churches, the largest of them in Superior, Wisconsin. For more than three decades it has been instrumental in maintaining worship and work in some tiny communities, while offering apprenticeship for first-call pastors straight from seminary under the capable leadership of an experienced pastor and many talented elders.

Moreover, as the ecology for faith development has grown to rely on ecumenical partners more than on competing with other branches of the Christian church, many Presbyterian churches are depending on Protestants of other backgrounds for "federated churches" and shared pastoral leadership. The Brandermill Presbyterian Church in suburban Richmond, Virginia, as several others in the denomination, actually began as a joint venture with United Methodists in the community.

Typically, as Presbyterian congregations have sprung up among immigrant populations in America's cities, host churches have provided space at little or no cost, sometimes sharing the expenses of pastoral leadership in the beginning. I am particularly aware of Korean and Twi-speaking Ghanaian congregations that have begun in that fashion, but colleagues speak of Bible fellowships and nascent churches of many ethnic origins that have origins in the hospitality and cooperation of several Presbyterian congregations.

With some churches struggling to maintain viability and others overflowing with talent and resources, it makes sense that increasingly large churches and small ones are in close relationships.

Congregations Large and Small in Partnerships

Some of the resources of congregations come from those of partners. In Indianapolis, Indiana, for example, Second Presbyterian Church, one of the largest in the PC(USA), is supporting the community ministry of Rachel Wann. Wann, who works with Second's deacons, the church's ministry teams, and community partnerships, also serves as the solo pastor for First Presbyterian Church, Edinburgh, Indiana, where she preaches, moderates the session, and provides leadership for pastoral care. First, Edinburgh, is tiny, with Sunday attendance of about twenty-five. The partnership, which benefits both churches, has existed for almost a full decade.

Pastors and elders from Giddings Lovejoy Presbytery tell of long-standing relationships between large and small Presbyterian churches in the Saint Louis area. Likewise, in Beckley, West Virginia, First Presbyterian Church has stayed in relationship with several of the congregations to which it "gave birth" generations ago.

Sometimes the effective agency of one Presbyterian can provide a resource for all the congregations in a presbytery—as teaching elder Barb Tesorero does for the Presbytery of Cincinnati.

Presbytery of Cincinnati: A Case Study

Each month, a newsletter in the Presbytery of Cincinnati highlights the work of one church project. Norwood Presbyterian's Baby Bear Closet; Reading-Lockland Presbyterian Church's Summer Program; One + One = Success for Bond Hill and West Cincinnati Churches; Every Child Succeeds, a Mission of Carmel Church; and CLASP (Children of Ludlow After School Program) are just a few of these projects. Each of these efforts—providing baby clothes, after-school tutoring and recreation, help for new mothers, summer programs, and many more—can receive the prayers and support of all the churches in the presbytery and volunteer assistance from anyone inspired to contribute.

The newsletter is a contribution itself of Barbara Tesorero, interim associate at Lakeside Presbyterian. She began the project hoping to generate mission and educational networking among congregations in the area. "I have always felt that things that bubble up are actually quite energizing for people," she explains. Her husband, Fran, says she serves as a "mission yenta," or matchmaker.

Barb Tesorero in Cincinnati, leaders at Harvey Browne and C. N. Jenkins, those at Second, Indianapolis, and First, Edinburgh—and lots of others—seek to offer food, clothing, shelter, comfort, and presence as Jesus directed followers to do. But these Presbyterian congregations are also frequently involved in seeking justice as well as mercy. According to the Bible, the two are inextricably bound. Care for individuals and prophetic, structurally oriented advocacy for a just society are more like the two sides of one coin—inseparable.

Congregational Resources for Seeking Justice

When I first offered reflections centering on Presbyterian congregational resources for mission, editors of the journal in which my essay appeared lamented that my perspective "forecloses the future prophetic response analogous to the moment when denominational leaders plunged into the struggle for civil rights in the 1960s."[2] Their perception of the location of the prophetic in denominational offices is one that I shared for some time. I have since come to recognize that congregations are the prime locations for effective prophetic response today. In fact, they may have been so in previous generations as well but simply did not perceive their witness in context.

On its Web site, Brown Memorial Park Avenue Presbyterian Church in Baltimore, Maryland, proclaims that it is "alive in the city and the world."[3] That is certainly true of leaders there who sponsored, lobbied for, and saw passed a $59-million bond bill to redevelop blighted neighborhoods in the city. Others from the church helped lead a coalition to join in worship at the National Cathedral, a Christian Peace Witness movement supporting the drawing down of troops in Iraq. An African American legislator from Brown Memorial introduced the Maryland Marriage Equity Bill in the state legislature. Pastor Andrew Foster Connors tells colleagues the marriage of an African American to a Caucasian wife would have been deemed "immoral and unnatural" as well as illegal just a few decades ago, as many consider gay marriage to be today. The congregation is also fostering eco-stewardship, Hua Kola Learning Camps and personal relationships with Native Americans in Dakota Presbytery, and peacemaking efforts locally and globally.

Members and elders at Western Presbyterian Church in Washington DC are also deeply involved in seeking justice. Members at Western filed suit in order to provide a Community Kitchen for the homeless, made national news as they won the right to keep that kitchen open, and now examine public policy and seek adequate laws for health care including for the vulnerable. They demonstrate on the Capitol steps for peace.

Menlo Park Presbyterian Church declares that its members are committed to "Serve the World: Seek Justice." "We believe that our response to issues such as human trafficking, disparity in education, and economic development is an essential part of our witness to Jesus Christ."[4] The mission statement also includes embodying compassion, equipping leaders, and discipling neighborhoods and nations.

Many Presbyterian pastors and sessions and other leaders in local churches take responsibility for social justice and community welfare. Kim Bobo, Executive Director of Interfaith Worker Justice, an independent nonprofit focusing churches on the rights of workers, wishes there were more. She tells of some that give particular support for those who do the most menial work in America—the dishwashers, garbage collectors, hotel workers, and seasonal agricultural employees.

Congregations on both sides of the Mexico-U.S. border support Presbyterian Border Ministries. Mission workers from the PC(USA) and from the Iglesia Nacional Presbiteriana de Mexico (INPM) at each of six sites coordinate the partnership between PC(USA) congregations and those of the INPM. Moreover, they are developing missions, congregations, and organized churches—evangelical and sensitive to the poor and to issues of justice. Numbers of PC(USA) congregations throughout the country are engaged in mission trips and support for clinics and schools in the border communities.

Several Florida congregations are involved right now in the Coalition of Immokalee Workers (CIW), seeking fair wages for tomato pickers and other agricultural workers. Vanderbilt Presbyterian Church in Naples, Florida, is just one of the nearby churches supporting the efforts. Other congregations and their pastors have assisted in the efforts for justice as CIW campaigns take place in New York City; Santa Ana, California; Madison, Wisconsin; and elsewhere.

According to John Wimberly, pastor of Western Presbyterian Church, congregational initiatives on behalf of peace and justice are most effective today. "There was a time when papers from the denomination, or the words of national leaders, made an impression in the political arena and in the world broadly speaking. Today, however, the involvement of people locally and in fluid networks makes the real difference."

Indeed the roles of "higher councils," presbyteries, synods, and the General Assembly that we used to call "judicatories," or "church courts," have changed. And they will doubtless keep changing in order to provide additional resources for Presbyterian work and worship in the future. As we explore the councils as resources for missional efforts and for justice concerns, we will find additional support for sustainability of a Presbyterian future.

Study Questions

1. At what times does your church summons its human and financial resources most effectively?
2. How do you network among congregations and in the community to be good stewards of congregational resources?
3. Are you engaged in partnerships with other congregations? What possibilities are available?

Chapter 7

Denominational Resources

As presbyteries, synods, and the general assembly arose in the United States, they provided resources for enhancing congregational life. They offered locations for pastors and sessions to network. All the worship and preaching afforded continuing education for pastors. And the councils made assignments of preaching points so nascent congregations periodically could receive sacraments and ultimately organize themselves on the frontiers. Granted, they also afforded locations for contention—whether and in what manner to proscribe theology and particular interpretations of certain biblical passages. But in the main, they convened ruling and teaching elders "decently and in order" so the worship and witness of Presbyterians could be enhanced.

In a sustainable Presbyterian future, the so-called higher councils are functioning in that manner once more. Most of those in positions of responsibility in national offices, as well as in many regional offices, are embracing the new ecology, already utilizing the new ways of connecting and locating resources for a coherent identity in the whirl of contemporary work and worship. The ones still seeking to function in patterns of traditional control and hierarchy are losing voice and location.

One of the most pleasant aspects of my research for this project has been the privilege of interviewing numbers of denominational officers. I have known some of them for many years. Others I met for the first time. I do respect all of them, for they have consented to serve the PC(USA) councils at a very difficult time, when national institutions are under siege, resources declining, and work demanding. Each reduction in staff nationally and regionally has brought dislocation and vocational disappointment for those released, additional responsibilities without increased remuneration for those remaining, and uncertainty for everyone. Many of those serving now are resourceful, creative, and disciplined in exercising their responsibilities.

When our *Presbyterian Presence* study was published in the early 1990s, leaders in most denominational offices at the time who bothered to read it were critical of it. Many took issue with our findings—that the PC(USA) sought to regulate Presbyterian congregational life and worship, that members join local churches rather than the PC(USA), and that most Presbyterians do not heed denominational pronouncements. In areas such as research services and theology and worship, denominational officers responded positively. They already sought to meet expressed needs of congregations and other Presbyterian groups. But in a number of other areas, the officers seemed to focus almost exclusively on their own programs and perspectives, expecting loyal Presbyterians at local levels to follow and support them.

How much has it changed? A lot.

A Flattened Hierarchy

The phrase *flattened hierarchy* partakes of oxymoron, like the phrase *jumbo shrimp*. A hierarchy requires some in the church to be higher than others. Further, officers among Reformed Christians are ordained to service—not privilege. Any ruling elder or teaching elder is equally empowered to represent our PC(USA) in the World Council of Churches as is the Stated Clerk of the General Assembly. What we have affirmed is that Christian councils, though they err, are more likely to discern God's will than individual Christians of whatever authority or office.

I first heard the expression flattened hierarchy from Linda Valentine, Executive Director of the General Assembly Mission Council. She said it with a knowing smile, well aware of its punch as a figure of speech. "We have come to a different place in the PC(USA)," elder Valentine observes. "We are still a large, complex system. But we now depend on networking and all kinds of communications in this flattened world we live in today. Many of us still carry images of some kind of church hierarchy, but it's just not that way now. It's been flattened, too."

Most of those now in national offices and many of those in presbyteries and synods, as Linda Valentine, perceive and welcome the new ecology and the new mission perspective. They not only support agency and adaptive leadership by teaching and ruling elders, in many cases they have refashioned our governing patterns and called people into the national offices to provide for congregational initiatives.

In a speech he regularly provides for councils and denominational committees, Gradye Parsons, Stated Clerk of the PC(USA), speaks of the new forms of church and the need for congregations to rethink what discipleship entails. He also speaks of the "extraordinary power of the ordinary life of the church." From Joplin, Missouri, where a tornado struck, he mused recently on the old coffee machines in a church basement, how they had supplied caffeine and refreshment for "church suppers, session meetings, Presbyterian Women gatherings" and now for church groups in mission trips to help in the rebuilding of the community after a disaster. He tells of the readiness of OGA offices to assist those who are teaching, preaching, providing pastoral care and seeking to embrace God's mission.[1]

In the area of global mission, Hunter Farrell, Director of World Mission for the PC(USA), has located an "Equipping the Church for Mission Office" at GAMC to support communications among a whole array of mission networks—groups of people who have interest in and experience with the peoples and churches in various countries throughout the world. Each mission network concentrates on a particular country or set of countries and the networks are clustered according to continental regions, with a catch-all cluster for the Kurdish Network and the Water Mission Network. So, for example, the Asia cluster contains six networks: China, Indian, Pakistan, South Pacific, Thailand, and Vietnam. The Central America-Mexico cluster contains networks for Costa Rica, El Salvador, Guatemala, Mexico, and Nicaragua.

The network for Israel-Palestine, in the Middle East cluster, communicates with churches and presbyteries concerning justice for refugees and nonviolent protests. The members share word of resources,

products from craftspeople in Palestine that can be purchased, and
even ways to make affirmative investments in the struggling Pales-
tinian economy. Through the network, many congregations in the
PC(USA) keep partnerships with churches, colleges, and councils
in Palestine and Israel. Lafayette-Orinda Presbyterian Church in
Lafayette, California, for example, relates to Ahli Arab Hospital and
the Atfaluna Society for Deaf Children, and members travel there as
they are able to help. Members of Memorial Presbyterian Church in
Midland, Michigan, and people from the Dar al-Kalima College in
Bethlehem visit back and forth, and the church provides resources
and scholarships for students in the music program of the college.
Similar relationships are afforded through most of the other mission
networks.

Tom Hay, Director of Operations for the Office of General Assembly, says that "We have been learning how to coach, recently, instead
of what page to cite where the *Book of Order* tells what to do." Most
welcome the possibility to offer denominational resources. We saw
this new style of leadership evident at a recent NEXT conference.

The NEXT Presbyterian Church Conference: A Case Study

We gather in the sanctuary of Second Presbyterian Church, Indianapolis, Indiana—350 of us coming in spring of 2011 to worship
and discuss what's NEXT for the Presbyterian Church. A group of
pastors issued the invitation, and they invited worship and discussion leaders from among their number and more broadly. The planners expected only about 100 to register, but more than three times
that are here. Volunteers from among the session, women's circles,
church staff, and lots of others provide hospitality and logistical support so everyone can think constructively about the future of our part
of the Christian family. What is God's mission today? How does the
church live into it? How can big and small churches work together?
How can we seek the welfare of the cities in which we live? How
can we engage faithfully in mission globally? What is our vocation?

Cynthia Bolbach, the Moderator of the General Assembly, is here,
as is the Vice-Moderator, Landon Whitsett. The heads of General
Assembly Mission Council and the Office of the General Assembly

attend as well as a score of other denominational officers. Linda Valentine praised the initiative of the pastors. "We enjoyed being participants," she reflected afterward, "sharing our ideas and wisdom among Presbyterians who seek to grow our church deep and wide."

Valentine recalls for us a 2008 mission consultation in Dallas at the Preston Hollow Presbyterian Church. She considers that a turning point in denominational thinking—a time leaders from the denominational offices, partner churches throughout the world, and many Presbyterian leaders in local congregations phrased the way global mission takes place today: "To be the church is to be one large mission society." She encourages local churches, partner churches, and denominational personnel to think collaboratively.

Participating actively in the next conference is Carmen Fowler, executive of *The Presbyterian Layman*, an independent periodical. She reported evenly on the conference, wishing that more had attended from the Presbyterian Coalition and Presbyterians for Renewal. She wrote, "The spirit of the event was positive, framed by beautiful Reformed, Word-centered worship and designed to promote genuine fellowship."[2]

Teaching elders, pastors working with their sessions, and other ruling elders initiated the NEXT conference. Denominational leaders gladly participated, welcoming the chance to collaborate with congregational leaders of every sort. Other meetings have been hosted by individual churches in the Fellowship of Presbyterians, and denominational leaders have attended there as well. Over the past several years, this shift in leadership style and attitude has become prevalent among many denominational executives (who, not incidentally, have quit using that word).

The PC(USA) Denomination Connections

In brief, the representative government of the PC(USA) grows from presbyteries electing commissioners to our General Assembly. At the center of denominational leadership is a General Assembly Mission Council (GAMC), charged with supporting the churches in ministry, inspiring and equipping leaders, and connecting various parts of the church. Support for evangelism; world mission; peace and justice efforts; church growth; racial, ethnic, and vocational concerns; and resources for theology and worship are all centered in GAMC.

Frequently we neglect to think about the other national offices of the PC(USA). The Office of the General Assembly, led by the Stated Clerk of the PC(USA), oversees legal aspects of our life together, keeps our records, and supports governance at every level of church life. The Presbyterian Foundation helps donors give effectively for ministries of the church and for other charitable purposes. The Presbyterian Investment and Loan Program assists congregations with low-cost loans for capital projects. The Presbyterian Publishing Corporation creates resources for Christian growth, scholarship, and inspiration. Finally, the Board of Pensions oversees investments, drawn largely from the contributions of congregations, to assure the health and welfare of missionaries, pastors, and other paid staff of churches.

Lots of other resources from General Assembly offices offer national and regional events and locations. Our three church-wide conference centers, Montreat, Stony Point, and Ghost Ranch, for example, provide numerous programs, and the national offices also provide staffing to help Presbyterian Women and Presbyterian Men. There are countless other national and regional resources in the church. In considering the future of the PC(USA), all these efforts and people should be included in the appraisal.

General Assembly commissioners elect committees to oversee the work of each of these denominational entities, with the exception of the conference centers. Committees and task forces elected by the General Assembly also address issues for the church such as the matter of the ordination of homosexuals and the new Form of Government. Another task force is seeking now to recommend ways to make our presbyteries and synods more effective for ministry and less costly to maintain in terms of time and money.

Denominational Resources for Congregations to Thrive

We have already named some ways the General Assembly offices and those of synods and presbyteries provide resources for local churches. The session of First Presbyterian, Burnsville, turned to their presbytery, Western North Carolina, for a grant to support redevelopment. The partnership, initiated by the session, is typical of those in presbyteries where leadership is cooperative and responsive in the new ecology of bubbling up ideas and mission. Many presbyteries and synods have special funds dedicated to such purposes. In addition, there are grants, loans, and other funds in several denominational offices—at the Presbyterian Investment and Loan Program, for example, and through the Office for Church Growth and Transformation.

Perhaps even more helpful than money for many congregations is information concerning the demography of the city or other area in which a church is located, which can be obtained from the cooperative staff in the Research Services area of the General Assembly Mission Council. Several congregations studied had asked concerning the results of census data for their communities and received help at little or no cost. Excellent books and pamphlets come from the work of staff, too.

When our Williamsburg Presbyterian Church celebrated a sesquicentennial recently, we received information and photos from the Presbyterian Historical Society to supplement our own cache of memorabilia for display. As First Presbyterian Church, Binghamton, and West Presbyterian in that city moved toward merger, both they and their presbytery received information concerning the legal consequences of various alternatives. In our day, information resources seem even more important than in previous times.

Resources offered through the Board of Pensions for Presbyterian pastors and members of the staffs of many congregations frequently go unnoticed. With assets of $7.1 billion, the PC(USA) pension fund is one of the strongest of nonprofits in the nation.[3] In addition to the regular, contractual benefits offered, church workers in many offices can receive counsel and advice, as can elders and other congregational leaders. Partnership programs are provided, including grants for some ministries and help with paying student loans when pastors are faithful in serving low-paying calls.

Leaders in churches are not shy about asking for resources from Presbyterian Disaster Assistance (PDA), a ministry of the GAMC and a highly functioning team of dedicated people who not only channel money to places and people in need when tsunamis, earthquakes, and floods occur but also help mission teams plan well for effective service. Likewise, most synods and many presbyteries collect funds and direct need where PDA says it can be effectively deployed.

As I write, PDA is concentrating efforts in Tuscaloosa, Alabama, where a deadly tornado recently ripped through the city. Representatives from the offices of the General Assembly and the Synod of Living Waters are being guided and housed by pastors and others from First Presbyterian Church and Brown Memorial Presbyterian Church, next to Stillman College. As churches did after Hurricane Katrina in New Orleans and the Gulf Coast, First Presbyterian in Tuscaloosa is setting aside space, and leaders from the two congregations and others are organizing efforts so congregation teams from across the country can come to help in the repairs and rehabilitation over the next five to six years.[4]

Digital resources from General Assembly and from regional offices are readily available for congregations as well. Our own Presbyterian Publishing Corporation is offering The Thoughtful Christian, an ecumenical educational resource on the Internet. The new *Feasting on the Word* lectionary-based curriculum likewise offers Christians of every description resources for spiritual formation and Christian education.

More than 350 Presbyterian Women are participating in an online, invitation-only circle, offering occasions for prayer, thoughts about the church, discussions, and round tables. Networks, virtual circles, curriculum, consulting—all these innovations result from denominational tinkering to assist local churches and individual Presbyterians.

Denominational Tinkering: Signs of Hope

The delightful part of re-imagining our structure is that most stated clerks and most regional and national officers have already discarded any impulses to control other bodies in the church. Members of the new Form of Government (nFOG) Task Force say that the Stated Clerk of the General Assembly and others from national offices coached them toward the reduction of regulations and dispensing with bureaucratic regulations as they drew up the document PC(USA) presbyteries ratified in 2011.

According to Paul Hooker, a general presbyter and a member of the nFOG Task Force, they wanted "to draft a polity that more clearly derived the way we govern the church (what the church *does*) from what we believe about the Church (what the Church *is*). To put it another way, our goal was to encourage the church to think theologically about its polity."

The task force also expressed hope that the nFOG would "declericalize" the PC(USA), more true to our Presbyterian origins. To work well, this way of governing together will require ruling elders and teaching elders alike to take responsibility in councils—much the way their forebears did in Reformation times and in the first decades of American Presbyterianism. Elders of both sorts will need to exercise agency.

Agency should come naturally to Presbyterian ruling elders. After all their ordination to church governance functions is on a par with that of teaching elders, more commonly known as pastors. In fact, as one elder pointed out to me recently, the Supreme Court of Iowa has recognized Presbyterian ruling elders as "ministers of the gospel within the meaning of the statute."[5]

Some presbyteries are re-forming radically to encourage agency among elders. The Presbytery of the James, led by Carson Rhyne, has moved to recognize and support purpose groups. Three or more people within congregations of the presbytery can apply to become one, covenanting for a specific time to focus on a special ministry. If funding is needed they can ask for presbytery assistance, with a three-year limit on particular grants of money. Additional participants in the purpose groups can include those from congregations in other denominations. Currently, twenty-four purpose groups are concentrating in areas such as new church development, maintaining stable families, global mission, youth ministry, the presbytery camp, hunger, and African immigrants.

Some congregations stick closely to denominational resources and rely chiefly on them. Presbyterian congregations, as other mainline churches, that identify closely with the tradition the denomination represents and inculcates are more prone to support the wider communities represented in that tradition, according to Nancy Ammerman. They are likely to "devote larger proportions of their budgets to the work of the extended organization of which they are a part."[6] Presbyterian congregations still depend on national offices for hymnals and much of their church school curricula, according to Ammerman. They also depend on denominational resources for advice concerning architecture, stewardship, and mission resources. More importantly, the narrative of congregations tied strongly to a mainline denomination is likely to lead to mission efforts consonant with national goals.

Even Nancy Ammerman, however, concludes that denominational identity "largely results from relationships and narrative practices, not authority, organization, or patterns of exchange."[7] In other words, the symbiosis between Presbyterian congregations and denominational offices still exists, but more informally than before.

Study Questions

1. In what ways is your congregation receiving resources from presbytery, synod, and the General Assembly offices?
2. What resources could help you witness more effectively? Who might help you secure them?
3. What should the next Presbyterian church be and do globally, nationally, and regionally?

Chapter 8

Presbyterian Seminaries and Colleges

*R*esources for a sustainable Presbyterian future certainly include those of the Presbyterian seminaries and many of the church-related colleges. Studies of mainline congregations and denominations seldom pay attention to these resources, and some actually blame the schools for the fracturing of the traditional Presbyterian ecology. True, the seminaries and colleges have consistently envisioned a broader, more-inclusive mission than just perpetuating Presbyterian identity and culture. Nevertheless, they have embodied both, and they now offer partnerships and support for Presbyterians who care to claim them.

Still it may seem ironic that as the ecology for Presbyterian faith development becomes more diffused and diverse, Presbyterian institutions of higher education are increasingly interested in supporting local churches and receiving support from them. Those of us with some years of experience in seeking symbiosis among schools and churches can recount times when many Presbyterian schools sought distance from local churches. Whatever the reason for the shifts, and there are doubtless multitudes, leaders in churches find the contemporary contexts opportune ones. This increasing zeal for collaboration bodes well for a thriving Presbyterian future. Consider a recent overture from a church in Roanoke, Virginia.

The Trent Symposium: A Case Study

The idea came from several sources in a Presbyterian congregation— a father grieving the death of his daughter, a pastor remembering good mentors who guided his development, and a willing session. The pastor and several elders had benefited already from the experience of a seminary in relating to the needs of local churches. Second Presbyterian Church in Roanoke, Virginia, began in 2008 to offer annually the Kittye Susan Trent Symposium for Newly Ordained Ministers.

John Trent lost his only daughter, Kittye Susan Trent. Grieving for her and wanting to honor her memory, he established a fund at Second "to promote theological education." George Anderson, senior pastor there, was already engaged in mentoring first-call pastors in ministry. He considered with the session a formal program with Union Presbyterian Seminary, his *alma mater* and a pioneer in self-directed, lifelong learning for pastors and other congregational leaders.

Ken McFayden, a professor at Union Presbyterian Seminary, was invited to be the codirector. Working with elders and others at Second—a university president, an owner of a construction company with special expertise in church finance, a partner in a Roanoke law firm, a district manager of a large company, and families willing to host meals for participants in their homes—they also enlisted Ed McLeod, pastor of First Presbyterian, Raleigh, a partner with George Anderson in their mutual continuing education, and professors from Union who taught leadership, preaching, and worship. Through the seminars of the symposium held at the church, the newly ordained ministers gain guidance from experienced ministers, professors, and laypeople with expertise in various areas of church and civic life.

The intense, small group of eight new pastors they select each year finds the experience crucial for their ministries. But benefits also accrue to the members and officers of Second Presbyterian Church, Roanoke, who now take some pride in their identity as a "teaching church."

"The Jewel in the Crown" of the PC(USA)

Michael Lindvall, pastor of the Brick Presbyterian Church in New York City and a noted author, declares that the Presbyterian seminaries are the "jewel in the crown" of the PC(USA). "No other denomination can draw on such a healthy and diverse mix of theological institutions to inform and enliven it," he tells Presbyterians across the country. Members of the seminary faculties and staffs are deeply involved in local church life in Presbyterian congregations and councils, even when some may belong in other parts of the Christian family.

Though all the seminaries and many of the colleges previously were under the control of the General Assembly or synods of Presbyterian denominations, almost all of them are now independently governed. In many respects their patterns of governance and relationships can be models for other, stressed institutions still owned by the church. The seminaries and many of the PC(USA)-related colleges mandate, according to their constitutions and bylaws, PC(USA) elders be on their boards. Some require a majority of board members to be Presbyterians. More important, all are willing and many are eager to form and sustain partnerships of mutual benefit to PC(USA) churches and the schools themselves.

Ten theological seminaries are integrally related to the PC(USA): Princeton Theological Seminary, Union Presbyterian Seminary, Pittsburgh Theological Seminary, San Francisco Theological Seminary, McCormick Theological Seminary, Louisville Presbyterian Theological Seminary, Columbia Theological Seminary, Austin Theological Seminary, University of Dubuque Theological Seminary, and Johnson C. Smith Theological Seminary. Two more seminaries, Auburn Seminary and Evangelical Seminary of Puerto Rico, are also more loosely related. Several other seminaries, especially Fuller Theological Seminary, Gordon Conwell Theological Seminary, and Duke Divinity School, have significant numbers of Presbyterian students and faculty. Even to introduce the complex histories and compositions of the schools would require at least another whole book. Suffice it to say they span the country, and they offer programs and partnerships already nourishing large portions of the PC(USA).

These Presbyterian seminaries are further along in recognizing and living into the new ecology than are most congregations and council leaders. Many of their faculty belong to other parts of the Christian church, and sometimes they include believers in others of the living religions as well. Yet, to open partnerships for mutual benefit they offer accessible and willing resources.

Dubuque has a special program in missional leadership and now offers a Master of Arts in the specialty. The director of the program, Professor Amanda Benckhuysen, has experience in new church development and proclaiming the gospel to those who have never before heard it. Those studying in the program learn about campus ministry, urban missions, and community development as well as ministry in more traditional congregations.

At Louisville Presbyterian Seminary, Professor Frances Adeney teaches evangelism and mission. A longtime Presbyterian mission coworker in Indonesia, she helps students relate the Christian gospel to those who profess other living religions, as well as those who profess no religious preference. Her Doors to Dialogue theme is more widely explored in the degree programs at Louisville. She teaches that, "We Christians have something to give in terms of our stories, in telling about Jesus."

Church Planting is one special degree program at Pittsburgh Seminary, where students spend a year engaged in a new church development project in the United States and another period of time studying a church planting effort in some other country and culture. One of the recent graduates, B. J. Woodworth, now collaborates in the program from the new church he helped to begin there in the city, The Open Door.

Columbia Seminary partnered with Presbyterian congregations in the Atlanta area to open a center for lifelong learning that gives lay leaders opportunities for certificates in Christian spiritual formation; youth ministry; and training for Korean, Spanish-speaking, and Portuguese lay leaders. For continuing education of pastors and the training of laypeople, their programs include travel seminars, focus on faith and the arts, and professional development. The president of Columbia, Steve Hayner, spends much of his time thinking with congregational leaders about resources and partnerships that can enhance their effectiveness. He speaks of Columbia trying to nourish "transformational leaders for God's global and missional Church," and by leaders it does not just meant pastors.

Union Presbyterian Seminary, where Second Presbyterian Roanoke turned for support in offering the Trent Symposium, opened a new campus in Charlotte, North Carolina, where students study part-time so that they can also serve churches as staff while they obtain degrees in ministry and Christian education. Union also has an Extended Campus Program in Richmond so that full-time church workers can study for mastery of the disciplines of Christian education.

Johnson C. Smith Seminary, as a part of the Interdenominational Theological Canter, offers distance education, appropriate for all but especially helpful for African American Presbyterians. Students from Austin Theological Seminary participate regularly with church folk from local congregations in a Kairos ministry at the prison in Gainesville, Texas. Princeton Seminary leads a national program in youth ministry. McCormick Seminary long has focused on the special ministry of urban churches.

These and many more emphases and programs at the individual seminaries give just a glimpse of the ministries they afford. And personally I have found all the seminaries responsive to requests for preachers, teachers, consultants, and partners for congregations that take the initiative to seek assistance.

In line with the new, ecumenical ecology, however, Presbyterians can expect seminaries of many traditions more readily to respond when opportunities offering mutual benefit are offered for their consideration. And Presbyterian-related colleges are equally good prospects as potential partners for mission and service. Consider two excellent colleges—Davidson in North Carolina, and Whitworth University in Spokane, Washington.

Charlotte Churches and Davidson College: A Case Study

Presbyterian colleges also respond affirmatively to the right invitation from Presbyterians in local churches. Don Davidson, a 1939 graduate of Davidson College, and his wife, Anne Stapleton Davidson, belonged at the time to First Presbyterian Church, Charlotte. The Davidsons asked leaders at the college and at their church about establishing an internship to help college students connect their community service with their Christian faith. They said they would welcome such a possibility. Subsequently, Covenant Presbyterian, Charlotte, was invited to join in the effort as well.

In 1989, the Stapleton Davidson Urban Service Internship program began to offer ten-week, paid summer internships for selected

Davidson students—five each year. The students work in social service agencies with marginalized populations—homeless neighbors, people in immediate financial crisis, and those recovering from addiction. They also meet weekly with the college chaplain, and with pastors of the sponsoring churches, to put their day-to-day experience into a biblical, theological, and broader context. The two churches also house the interns in the homes of members, and the students worship at their host churches, sometimes helping lead portions of services.

Students in the program speak in glowing terms of their experiences. One intern recently wrote, "I learned new lessons about Christ's love." Another said, "It made me believe that the church's job in this world is first and foremost to care for our fellow human beings, especially those who suffer the most." And Corrine Hester, who reported on her experience during 2010 working in a men's shelter and a food pantry, says, "I spent my summer getting to know the men that the world had taught me to fear. I spent my summer getting to know the men Jesus knew—the sick, the lonely, the outcasts, and the criminals."

The experience so affected Covenant Church that the congregation has now begun a similar program in partnership with nearby Queens University in Charlotte. The pastors tell of the benefits for those in the congregation, having members of affluent families learn of the plight of the poor through conversation with students who reside with them for the summer. And the student interns can "serve as advance scouts" for new social ministries the church is considering.

Westminster Presbyterian and Whitworth University in Spokane, Washington: A Case Study

Begun in 1991, a partnership between Westminster Presbyterian Church and Whitworth students and faculty turned a former crack house into a residence for students and a center for providing basic social services. Spokane's West Central area is recognized as the poorest neighborhood in the state of Washington, and the needs of the residents and opportunities for ministry are abundant. Five students at the school and the pastor of the church initiated the project, which continues twenty years later to offer resources for the community and indelible learning for the students involved. Now numbers of other partnerships link churches and Whitworth students, where during the fall semester of 2010 more than 1,800 students gave more than 12,500 hours of service in Spokane. Almost 600 of the 3,000 students altogether engaged in service learning.

Dale Soden, a PC(USA) teaching elder and Professor of History at Whitworth, is charged with directing the school's Weyerhaeuser Center, which offers a Certificate in Lay Ministry. This program, now available online, offers basic training for those who want to serve as Certified Lay Pastors, especially in the Washington/Alaska Synod. He speaks fondly of other partnerships over the years—relationships between African American and white churches, rural church resources, and training for church musicians—all useful and constructive while financial resources permitted.

Schools Help in Cobbling a Faithful Presence

In these and other similar situations, partnerships grew from Presbyterians seeking to be faithful, Presbyterians who belonged both in a congregation and the community of a seminary or college. More illustrations come to mind. In each case, the mission and nurture for a congregation overlaps with the mission of a school and its desire for excellent education of students. There is a distinctively Presbyterian flavor to such mutually enriching efforts.

Hastings College, in Nebraska, also focuses on service learning for students with opportunities that strengthen congregations—Presbyterian and other—in the Great Plains. One hundred and more Presbyterian pastors from Nebraska and surrounding states come to Hastings each summer for continuing education supported by the Omaha Seminary Foundation. A winter retreat for pastors and other leaders of congregations, jointly sponsored by Hastings and Omaha, offers another channel for suggesting areas of interest and needs of the churches, according to David McCarthy, chaplain and a professor there.

Austin College in Sherman, Texas, was founded by Presbyterian missionary Daniel Baker. It sponsors an Activators program, offering students to plan and lead ministry events. Westminster College, New Wilmington, Pennsylvania, hosts a mission conference that has, for one hundred years, been instrumental in highlighting Presbyterian mission and the work of other Christians globally. Other schools have programs in place related to church life, and doubtless every one of them would welcome opportunities to enhance the learning experiences of students.

On the other side of the ledger, schools frequently afford churches ample numbers of elders and deacons, musicians, youth directors, and Sunday school teachers. Particularly those congregations that host campus ministry programs find significant benefits in the quality of worship and work afforded by students and faculty. University Presbyterian Church in Chapel Hill, North Carolina, sponsors one of the finest campus ministry programs, with the University of North Carolina campus right across Franklin Street from the church building. The ministry is governed by a board that includes members from other Presbyterian churches in the vicinity. And the students who come are most frequently, but not always, Presbyterians. Pastor Robert Dunham says the church profits enormously from the infusion of talent, zeal, and intellectual vigor of students and faculty who belong to the church.[1]

At another University Presbyterian Church, this one in Seattle, Washington, hundreds of college-age folks meet together on Tuesday nights for worship. Small groups, mission efforts at Christmas, short-term and year-long international ministries, and other leadership opportunities are offered for students from many area colleges. The invitation, "You don't need to consider yourself a Christian to come," is part of a welcoming video on the Web site.[2] The campus ministry is related to the Young Life College and the Ascent Network, Christian affiliations that stretch across the country in a variety of schools and universities.

Similarly, Shandon Presbyterian Church in Columbia, South Carolina, has assumed major responsibilities for the Presbyterian campus ministry on the home campus in that city. Leaders at the church say congregations in other towns and cities in South Carolina are also sponsoring work with college students.

At our Presbyterian Church in Williamsburg, a Wesfel (Westminster Fellowship) group meets regularly on Sunday evenings.

Students from William and Mary also run a campus kitchen, cooking and delivering meals for needy families and individuals. Other students care for infants in the nursery, sing in the choir, or simply attend worship at the church, which seeks to provide hospitality for everyone. And faculty members, as well as members of the administration and staff, are vital in our work and worship.

Each of the campus ministries and partnerships is unique. But all help young Christians find their way joyfully in faith development. Not surprising are the testimonies of leaders in the congregations that they receive much more from the ministries than they give to them. And these resources assist Presbyterians in giving voice to our Christian faith. And as we cobble a Presbyterian identity today, we both fashion our emphases in Christian faith and interpret them as we find meaning in practicing the faith.

In the previous, traditional ecology we Presbyterians were not obliged to state what we believe, though many of us could do so eloquently. Presbyterians had learned to give voice to their faith through years of family devotions, Sunday school classes, and testimonies in Presbyterian mission efforts. Presbyterian colleges taught Reformed Christianity predominantly. Presbyterian seminaries offered primarily Presbyterian perspectives on Bible, theology, polity, and history. We could invite people to enter the Presbyterian ecology at many access points, and for many reasons they joined Presbyterian churches and learned incrementally of Reformed practices.

But by the same token, Presbyterians three and four generations ago did not have to articulate our faith as we do today. In a Presbyterian hospital owned by the church, staffed heavily with Presbyterian doctors and nurses, with volunteer workers from Presbyterian churches nearby, it was apparent to most that everyone was involved because they believe the gospel of Jesus Christ. In a Presbyterian school of past generations, the same conclusion could be easily drawn.

Today, many who join Presbyterian congregations have little idea how to phrase their growing Christian faith, how to grow in a life of prayer, how to grow in generosity and ability to minister in the name of Jesus Christ. And those of us who are well-experienced in Presbyterian life need to be able to speak of our faith to help new believers. We need a Christian vocabulary for our own time, and we need confidence as well as competence in proclaiming the gospel.

Study Questions

1. In what ways is your church in partnership with Presbyterian seminaries and colleges?
2. Do you see ministries that might elicit a partnership with a seminary or college, Presbyterian or other?
3. Can your congregation be a community of faith that helps to educate pastors, educators, and other church leaders? How?

Chapter 9

Voicing Our Faith as Presbyterians

Someone posted words in our Sunday school classroom: "Preach the Gospel at all times. If necessary, use words." This seems to be one of those times!

Providentially, many Presbyterians are experienced in phrasing the faith, telling the gospel story. Many others are practicing the skills and learning the story to tell it in winsome fashion.

Consider the Ormond Beach Presbyterian Church.

Ormond Beach Presbyterian Church: A Case Study

The video on the Ormond Beach Presbyterian Church Web site begins by talking about change—changes in people and changes in the world.[1] It explains that while the Christian gospel does not change, ways of expressing it change today. The images are ones of people changing as they age.

The voice-over speaks of a church. "It is not just a building. It is a community that reaches out beyond its walls, to its own neighborhood and to communities beyond." The photos are of people constructing a house, with an image of the world rising behind the roofers and the carpenters.

A member, Will Akers, tells of the church building Habitat houses. The pastor, Mike Foley, and several more men and women of various ages are featured as the video continues with an exploration of the Greek word *koinonia*. "The early church was frequently described as a *koinonia*, a Greek word translated to mean fellowship, partnership, and joint-ownership. It's also used for words unity, sharing, giving, acceptance, and belonging."

Pastor Foley talks of people growing "when the Spirit of the living God is moving in the midst of that community." He names the singing of hymns, the praying, the preaching, the "breaking of bread." The narrator adds, "and if you come early, there's fellowship around the coffee table . . . and donuts too."

"We invite you to be part of our community, to experience the feeling of belonging, and to know the joy of being served, and the satisfaction of serving others." The narrator again adds, "Come, join our community of faith, hope and love, . . . a community of changed lives and a personal relationship with Jesus Christ." Finally, you can hear the choir sing Hal Hobson's "We Sing the Mighty Power of God."

Credits at the close show that the video was the work of the Evangelism Committee. The gentle invitation of the video is echoed in the recent story of the congregation and Pastor Foley's leadership style. "The Ormond Beach church was pretty conflicted six years ago," Pastor Foley remembers. "It had grown in 40 years to about 750 and then declined to about 250. People were pretty dispirited. Our session read together a book about the urgency of becoming a transformed church. Then we jumped at the opportunity to join some other congregations in the Presbytery of Central Florida in the Acts 16:5 Ministry as offered by Stan Ott."

Ormond Beach leaders began to focus not so much on gaining members as on making disciples—of both those in the church and those they invited to join. "At first, people's eyes would cross when we talked about evangelism. It was hard for them to see what was involved. So we worked for several months with an artist, who finally represented for us what we were trying to do. He painted panels we mounted in the sanctuary. Five of them. One shows a person free, having broken a binding chain. A second shows people rejoicing and a hand with a seedling. A third is the back of a shadowy figure of Jesus Christ, with the Presbyterian cross symbol. A fourth is the other hand with the seedling and someone leaving the boat, as Peter did in faith. The fifth shows disciples leaving their nets to follow Jesus."

Pastor Foley relies on the representations of evangelism as he preaches. "I say that the work is 'in the water,'" he explains. "The fish don't just jump in the boat very often. . . . We invite people to share their stories of faith gently, speak as you can without being obnoxious. We used 'testimony' in worship for a while, but now it seems people are ready to invite others to experience faith."

"We are growing more competent in evangelism as we also grow more in mission and outreach," he continues. "Our church decided to build a Habitat house to celebrate our fiftieth anniversary. Even in the hard economic times, with so many Floridians on fixed incomes as retirees, we raised the eighty thousand dollars necessary in just twelve weeks. And we're stretching with others in a Helping Hands Day—150 of us old people and young volunteering around the community. We're supporting Presbyterian missionaries, doing lots to reach out."

Resources for Words to Phrase the Gospel

The Ormond Beach Presbyterian Church is just one of several congregations in Central Florida Presbytery engaged in the Acts 16:5 Ministry led by E. Stanley Ott,[2] a teaching pastor at the Vienna Presbyterian Church in Vienna, Virginia. More than three hundred congregations in the PC(USA) are similarly engaged in the three-year process of becoming disciples and learning to make disciples. First Presbyterian, Burnsville, which we visited in chapter 2, participates in the Acts 16:5 ministry, as do several other congregations in that presbytery. Several congregations in the Presbytery of the James participate also, and they formed one of the purpose groups discussed in chapter 7.

Scores of other congregations are either following programs designed to help them grow in faith or help them proclaim the Christian faith so others can accept it. Processes and studies offered by Graham Standish, Martha Grace Reese, and Anthony Robinson are among the most popular, and among the most constructive. All of them center in prayer, Bible study, and small groups sharing their own stories of faith.

Graham Standish, pastor of the Calvin Presbyterian Church in Zelienople, Ohio, teaches about becoming a blessed church, the title of one of his books.[3] Readers can learn from the experience of those at Calvin Presbyterian about how to be more open to the work of the Holy Spirit. As with Acts 16:5, the Blessed Church programs focus on spiritual life and use small groups for discernment and increasing expectations.

Bryant Harris, pastor of the Mars Hill Presbyterian Church in Acworth, Georgia, recently told of using the work with incoming deacons and ruling elders. The study "has had a positive impact . . . as we become more open to God's presence, purpose and power in our midst." Congregations in other denominations in the United States and Canada depend on the works of Standish as well.[4]

Members of the South Highland Presbyterian Church in Birmingham, Alabama, and the First Presbyterian Church of Gainesville, Florida, speak warmly of the studies offered by Martha Grace Reese, whose ordination is both in the United Church of Christ and in the Disciples of Christ. Several of those telling of their experience in prayer and evangelism say they previously had little exposure to the Christian faith. One young man said he had never read the Bible before. Use of prayer partners and small groups, again, is vital in this disciplined form of study.[5]

This Lilly Endowment-supported program involves more than 15,000 congregations in 49 denominations, including several hundred Presbyterian churches. The program offers first a leader's study, *Unbinding the Gospel,* with a small group of congregational officers and informal leaders. Next comes an "all-church saturation study," *Unbinding Your Heart.* This is a six-week course with sermons, prayer groups, and daily exercises for everyone. *Unbinding Your Church* is a third book in the series to support leaders during the saturation time for church members. Finally, *Unbinding Your Soul* foments discussions about evangelism and telling stories of faith. Coaching for those congregations that undertake a full three-year cycle is part of the grant-supported effort, so the costs to a local church are reduced considerably.

Another ordained UCC pastor, Anthony Robinson, has been working with many Presbyterian churches across the country. His seminal *Transforming Congregational Culture* helps leaders think clearly about the life of faith and phrasing the Christian gospel in our time. His more recent *Changing the Conversation: A Third Way for Congregations* helps leaders in their churches redirect administration from secular to more appropriate gospel-oriented ways of work and worship.[6]

Myers Park Presbyterian Church in Charlotte, North Carolina, asked Robinson to help them rethink their outreach and evangelism. According to Pastor Steve Eason, he helped them move from being membership-centered to a focus on being disciples and growing disciples. "Tony helped us return to Christian core values," Eason explains. "We began to see ourselves more in missional terms— seeking to join the world in God's mission rather than trying to get all the world to join the church."

Doing Your Own Evangelism

Still others take insights from Standish, Ott, Reese, Robinson, and more but "do their own thing." At the Pioneer Memorial Presbyterian Church in Solon, Ohio, the fastest growing congregation in the Presbytery of the Western Reserve, copastors Kerri and Jeff Peterson-Davis use small listening groups to identify the interests and dreams of members. They hosted Graham Standish for his time with the presbytery, and members of the session read his book together. They focus on Bible study and prayer, as Ott and Reese suggest. But they credit the public presence of congregational leaders, their excellent preschool, their immersion in mission, and the use of media such as blogs and their Web site for attracting the individuals and families who visit and join.

They post testimonies on the Web site home page: "I felt welcomed from the first time I visited. I love that there are so many children at Pioneer and such a caring environment for them."[7] Kerri Peterson-Davis's blog, "I Wonder Where This Road Will Take Us," tells of faith development, offers good books to read, and provides some resources for the sermons she preaches.[8]

They delight in the ability of Pioneer to be "quick to give permission" when people want to do things. Kerri says, "We go through channels here, but we do not let things stop in those channels."

Presbyterian pastor Foster Shannon, in a project examining fifteen growing Presbyterian congregations in California and Hawaii, located this emphasis on evangelism and outreach in every one of them. He also found them all proud of their ministries of various sorts, led by pastors who preached, taught, and provided pastoral care competently. All fifteen churches, though quite varied in size and concentrations, were quite confident and even eager to speak of their work and worship.[9]

While the present study is not focused on membership growth, certainly the equipping of the saints for the work of ministry today requires teaching Presbyterians how to speak of the faith and the Christian gospel. Presbyterian congregations are receiving good resources, and it behooves us to speak of what we do and to invite others to join. You might say, we need to brag modestly.

Presbyterians Bragging Modestly

On its Web site, the Bethel Presbyterian Church in Kingston, Tennessee, concludes a modest statement about its worship—"traditional style, but we also include time to warmly welcome visitors as well as an opportunity to share individual prayer requests"—with the following:

> New members tell us that they chose Bethel because they found us to be a warm, supportive congregation with intellectually challenging preaching from a caring pastor, all of us eager to engage in discussion and committed to doing God's work in the world.[10]

Such a straightforward testimony describes the response of a new member, but it also invites others with similar perspectives and desires to visit the church. After all, in our culture many, particularly younger people, have almost no concept of the freedom in Jesus Christ, the assurance of God's care, and the hope of eternal life. For individuals to be able to speak freely of their faith and to invite others to share life in Christ is one necessary part of the sustainable future for Presbyterians. Structuring congregational work and worship in winsome ways is yet another, the corporate side of evangelism.

Study Questions

1. Can you tell others about your Christian faith in words that invite them to share in it? How do you draw on the words of Scripture? Your own experience in prayer?
2. Is your church a place where people feel free to share faith, doubts, and prayers for themselves and others? How can you practice prayer and testimony?
3. Whose example helps you speak of your Christian faith?

Chapter 10

Emerging Possibilities

The new Presbyterian ecology and our new ways of making connections, entering into partnerships, and drawing on resources, all multiply the prospects for a viable Presbyterian future. In addition to the five ingredients already named and explored, we find evidence of several more that may be emerging to thicken the new ecology.

Certainly Presbyterians are experimenting more today with creative forms of congregational life. We are also more tolerant today of those who follow other religious traditions, perhaps even growing in faith from relationships among Christians, Jews, Muslims, Buddhists, Hindus, and those with other faiths. Some congregations, networking in presbytery, synod, and General Assembly settings but more frequently in issue-oriented organizations and movements, are gaining spiritual nourishment from what we frequently call *environmental stewardship*—exercising actively to preserve and care for God's whole creation and the life forms in it. And some relate integrally to the arts and to creative artists in various art forms.

These are only some of the other elements in the new ecology that may enhance faith development among Presbyterians today. Providentially, excellent books and blogs are addressing all these and many more that merit consideration.

Speaking of emerging, Presbyterian new church developments especially are drawing on insights from an emergent and emerging church movement. They may also function as leaven for the loaf of the whole church, lending enthusiasm and creative ideas for more settled and long-standing congregations. And they shed light on other emergent elements in the new ecology.

Consider the Covenant Community Church, recently chartered in Louisville, Kentucky.

The Covenant Community Church

The Covenant Community Church (C.C.C.) in urban Louisville, Kentucky, worships in the James Lees Presbyterian Church building every Sunday evening. As the worshipers gather, they greet one another with hugs and handshakes. The old church building follows the modified Akron Plan, with semi-circles of rows of sanctuary pews focused on a large semi-circle chancel with a central pulpit and large Communion table. The elaborate, upholstered pulpit chairs are pulled to the sides—hundred-year-old furnishings, shop worn and dusty. The fellowship hall is the partially finished basement. Youth and meeting rooms are up the staircase. The building is far from the focus of this faith community. Leaders explain they want to recycle space; they would rather give for mission than for maintenance of a building, though they pay a modest rent.

Several pastors are present with spouses, with families, or by themselves. Some are retired, and a few serve churches elsewhere. This time of day affords them a chance to worship alongside their children and spouses, though they may preach and teach in another congregation on Sunday mornings. Worship is led by a worship team, only a portion of whom hold theological degrees.

The congregants, mostly white, include single folk and families. They welcome children to move about and encourage different leaders to share elements in worship. At one of the services I attended, the convening pastor/teaching elder, Jud Hendrix, offered the prayers of the people. The sermon was preached by Rachel Parsons, who keeps a covenant here and also leads Kenesis Communities, a presbytery ministry for young adults at the University of Louisville and people in that area. We sing to a guitar, a banjo, and a piano, bluegrass style, indigenous in this area of the Kentucky Bluegrass. We sing new hymns and Taizé chants and hear a soulful anthem. Several congregants make announcements informally, including word of another forming intentional community and of a public demonstration at city hall. We celebrate Communion together, as C.C.C. does every week.

Every Sunday after worship, a potluck dinner, called a Communion meal, draws congregants into fellowship and the sharing of food. Near Eastern dishes are served on this occasion, provided by one of the supported refugee families. Various desserts and salads augment the fare. Hosts conscientiously use environmentally righteous utensils and dinnerware.

C.C.C. resembles other Presbyterian churches in many ways, but it also experiments a lot with forms of worship and ministries. People here make annual covenant commitments that exceed membership promises in most churches—commitments that require financial and time commitments to the ministries they undertake. They belong to Intentional Communities, which together constitute the C.C.C. The Intentional Communities also meet weekly and support ministries in the Louisville area as well as political lobbying. One focuses on low-income homeowners with maintenance issues. Another explores the relationships of food and justice worldwide. Another plans worship.

C.C.C. began when two associate pastors at established congregations in Louisville, Hendrix and Elizabeth Kaznak, preached sermons on disciplined ways to know Jesus today. Friends of both shared the two sermons and encouraged the two to work together. A small group started an informal community with high expectations on participants. The church has evolved from that initial experience. Elizabeth Kaznak now directs the Kentucky Refugee Ministries, a close partner with C.C.C. in providing support for immigrants.

Several of the pastors who make covenants in the C.C.C. tell of their joy and satisfaction at being able to participate in the worship and mission. Others in the area presbyteries and more broadly in the church speak with enthusiasm about the example the C.C.C. sets for coherent Presbyterian work and worship.

Presbyterian Emergent Churches

The C.C.C. takes its direction from the special vocations of those who make covenant there, from the leadership of several talented and committed pastors and ruling elders, and from its context in urban Louisville. But it also resembles congregations in the emergent church movement, an ecumenical and particularly Anglo-American

Christian response to postmodern (and some say postevangelical) culture. What began as an effort to reach younger people using popular culture, media, and nontraditional worship and mission styles evolved quickly into an umbrella label for new forms of church with emphases on being disciples and making disciples.

Some characteristics of emergent churches include listening with fresh ears to the teachings of Jesus and practicing the radical hospitality he taught; establishing high thresholds for participation such as living in community; quickly adapting to local needs and resources; valuing Christian practices over theological precision; and being friends and colleagues in ministry with believers of other living religions. In fact, much of the energy in the movement is over against prevailing institutions, conservative and liberal, frequently seen as bureaucratic, closed, and moribund—part of the fast-dissolving modern world.

Presbyterian denominational leaders have invited Brian McLaren, Phyllis Tickle, and other leaders in the emergent church movement to speak at conferences and staff retreats about their "generous orthodoxy," which is open to constructive relationships with other religions. These proponents of a new kind of Christianity emphasize that older forms of church are not disappearing while new forms emerge. And they teach that emergent congregations in more traditional parts of the Christian family, such as the PC(USA), offer attractive examples for everyone. They point to turnarounds, in which dry bones take on new life. Many of the tools for new church development provided by the PC(USA) now reflect this perspective.

Many Gifts, One Spirit

The apostle Paul taught Christians in Corinth that individuals have many different gifts, but the same Holy Spirit quickens all of them. In the same fashion, many congregations draw on differing contexts and resources, but they share a liveliness in spirit and draw on gifts of the Spirit in similar ways.

In recent years, Presbyterian (and other) congregations in the Philadelphia area have collaborated to support the Broad Street Ministry (BSM), a Christian community that "cherishes creativity," "nurtures artists," and "extends inclusive and radical hospitality" in the middle of the arts district in the city.[1] The worship services on Sunday evenings at Broad Street, no-barriers dinners spurring community involvement, their intern program for seminarians and college-age students, youth immersion programs, and their educational events for pastors and other leaders are staffed by more than a score paid and volunteer workers. In 2009, Bill Golderer, founding pastor of the BSM, also became the pastor of the Arch Street Presbyterian Church, an urban congregation dating from Revolutionary times. The active partnership of Arch Street and BSM extends to sharing other pastors, Becky White Newgren and Mike Pulsifer among them. Excellent musicians, including J. Donald Dumpson, a world-renowned director of choral events, command respect among the arts communities in the city while they enrich the worship and work of the churches.

New Creation Presbyterian Church in O'Fallon, Illinois, near St. Louis, is another new church development listening to insights from the emergent church movement. Meeting in the worship and Christian education spaces of an Episcopal congregation, they hold worship services on a Saturday evening once a month and have a family-oriented service with children's church for ages 4–10 every week. Almost thirty have made covenant in that community, and another forty and more are friends who attend and share in the ministry.

Their pastor, Christian Boyd, who works for the Presbytery of Giddings-Lovejoy, tells of the high commitment of those in covenant—their giving of time and financial support. No offering is taken during worship, for instance. A basket is placed in the back of the sanctuary so people who want to give are able to do so. But those in covenant try to be good stewards of God's gifts in all they do, providing necessary money as well as time and talents in community enterprises. They receive regular requests for special mission funds as those in covenant perceive needs and opportunities.

Providence Presbyterian Church in Providence, Rhode Island, grows from the 1986 merger of two struggling congregations. As copastors Joe Miller and Chris Foster led the redevelopment, and when Miller retired, David Watermulder was called to share leadership with Foster. In the changing neighborhood, membership grew to include people of Asian, Latino, and African heritage. With Watermulder's facility in several languages and his experience in international service, the church attracted immigrant Christians, especially from Kenya and Ghana. Worship attendance has more than tripled in the last few years, and the giving from the church is generous for regional and global mission as well as for local efforts in the Mt. Hope neighborhood.

Providence Presbyterian, near Brown University, Rhode Island School of Design, Rhode Island University, and other colleges, now enjoys a college fellowship, hosts a college brunch monthly, and invites students for service opportunities. Brown faculty member Matt and his wife, Marianne Harrison, both recent graduates of Brown, lead the group.

These, and scores of other new church communities and fluid Presbyterian groups, are perhaps reshaping our PC(USA) and certainly have already changed our previously rigid models for new church development. A decade ago and more, presbyteries and the denominational offices expected new churches to grow from the purchases of land in strategic locations, the calling of pastors with special skills and training in church planting, and a vision of hundreds of congregants worshiping in new buildings within a few years. This formula, modified little from sometimes-successful version of the 1950s, rarely resulted in new, self-sufficient congregations in the 1990s or more recently.

All these experimental congregations and others named by those interviewed for this book share communal expectations among members. They invite people to discipleship, and they outline terms of common commitment—giving of money, time, and talents; willingness to engage in regular prayer and Bible study; taking opportunities for mission and service; and proclaiming the gospel in word as well as deed. Indeed, these new Presbyterian congregations share what students of congregational life term "high thresholds." Frequently they speak of "growing disciples," not just gaining members.

High-Threshold Congregations

For decades, long before an emergent church paradigm arose, some Presbyterian congregations maintained high thresholds for those who belonged. As I grew up in Memphis, Tennessee, the Balmoral

Presbyterian Church there began with founding pastor Vernon Hunter inviting neighbors to help form such a church. Memorial Drive Presbyterian Church in Houston, Texas, long expected that giving for benevolences would match or surpass annual operational expenses. Such disciplined participation is exceedingly rare in a consumer culture such as ours. But a sustainable Presbyterian future contains models of such generosity and Christian maturity.

The Trinity Presbyterian Church in Harrisonburg, Virginia, is one high-threshold church of note, one of a number that could be examples for all Presbyterians. Organizing minister Donald Allen and a band of committed Presbyterians began a congregation in 1962 in a house. From the one coffee house church, focused on nurture, fellowship, worship, and mission, came the continuing reliance on house churches as ministry escalated.[2]

To name just one example from their history of mission and witness, they became conscious in the 1970s of the needs of mentally challenged people in the area. A Community House Church at Trinity began a summer day camp for children who could not attend regular camps. One of the members of Trinity soon was appointed a member of the state board of the Association for Retarded Citizens, and the church lobbied for laws more supportive of people with such needs.

Today a vibrant church of more than 160 members offers the resources of a congregation many times its size.[3] House churches concentrate on an African partnership, peacemaking efforts to build community, health concerns, a clothes closet, the environment, and campus ministry. Pastor Ann Reed Held describes their annual meeting to select participants in the house churches as a draft night, a meeting in which leaders of each group select those who will join them based on listed preferences from everyone.

The profiles of these high-threshold congregations and new church developments, as emergent churches of every hue and flavor, suggest another element in the new ecology of American life. Congregations with higher expectations of all members may become even more significant for our new Presbyterian ecology in the future. As yet, however, few Presbyterian congregations call attention to their efforts in this direction.

The churches named and described in this chapter all warm to the faithful in others of the living religions. Is this also a mark of the new ecology?

Hospitality toward Believers in Other Living Religions

Annie Lamont, iconoclastic writer of the people, speaks of her eclectic Presbyterian spirit. "I wear something on my wrist that one would not expect a Presbyterian woman to wear: a thin red cotton cord that was blessed by the Dalai Lama, and given to me by my Buddhist friend Jack Kornfield."[4]

My research makes me wonder. It seems many, if not most, Presbyterians would appear to welcome a wristband blessed by a Buddhist leader. Many Presbyterian churches, even ones that identify themselves as conservative or evangelical, offer yoga and Tai Chi classes and groups that practice transcendental meditation, for example. When asked, the leaders of these classes speak only of benefits from the Buddhist practices.

While not yet ready to include hospitality toward believers in others of the living religions as another element in the new Presbyterian ecology, I am wondering if it might not soon become one. Certainly in every one of the new church developments and high-threshold congregations explored, I find interest in and dialogue with members of other living faiths among the stated programs and ministries.

Recent works by Robert Putnam and David Campbell argue, moreover, that religious congregations in America offer greater resources for societal cohesion and constructive citizenship than any other institutions, and today they reduce prejudice and increase religious tolerance among us all. They claim religious congregations have always generated what they call "social capital," as do other nonprofit groups. Social capital is the give-and-take, the trust built by participation in social networks. It grows as people in congregations bond with others who share similar faith and values.

But they claim that today social capital also grows as people in congregations build bridges with those who are different, whose lives and values are not the same. Both "bonding social capital" and "bridging social capital" come from congregational life, they assert.

A diminution of bonding social capital seems to be represented in the thinning of the traditional Presbyterian ecology, while the growth in bridging social capital comes from the diversity represented in the new ecology for Presbyterian faith development. Putnam and Campbell term the new situation "the Aunt Susan Principle." They find that most Americans today have intimate, mostly familial acquaintance with people of other religions. "We all have an Aunt Susan in our lives, the sort of person who epitomizes what it means to be a saint, but whose religious background is different from our own."[5]

They also confirm the insights of Robert Wuthnow who found that personal friendships between people of differing faiths leads to higher opinions of those religions.[6] Putnam and Campbell joke that this may be termed the "My Friend Al Corollary" to the Aunt Susan Principle. Gaining new friends who belong to a differing group leads to a higher estimation of the group altogether.[7]

In many communities, Presbyterian women (some men, too) have formed faith clubs with Jewish and Muslim believers. As in the case of the Kentucky Refugees Ministries, closely related to the Covenant Community Church, many of the resettling families and individuals come from countries in which Islam is practiced by most citizens. Recently, in one Presbyterian church, I was alerted that some members of the Shiite Muslim family they sponsored might well be taking Lord's Supper with the congregation. "They asked if they could join their church family in the sacrament," I was told, "and our session responded positively to their request." The wife and mother in that family is actively gathering a group of women—Christian, Jewish, and Islamic—to form yet another faith club for "daughters of Abraham to learn together of their faiths and commonality."

Putnam and Campbell find that 79 percent of mainline Protestants believe "persons not of my faith can go to heaven."[8] Presbyterian Panel findings show less robust majorities of Presbyterians thinking in this fashion, but a significant shift in that direction. And their statistics show also a trend toward more Presbyterian involvement in environmental issues and care for creation.

Environmental Stewardship and Support of the Arts

The Village Presbyterian Church in Prairie Village, Kansas, devotes one ministry to environmental justice. Granted, it is a large congregation. But even so, their 427 tons of recycled paper since 2003, the trees saved, and the $8,300 they received from recycling efforts make a statement about what a church can do. They bought durable, melamine dinnerware, and they figure it saves money and it certainly reduced use of Styrofoam. They engage in education and advocacy concerning environmental stewardship, give out compact fluorescent bulbs after worship, buy eco-palms, use native plants, drip irrigation, and in a host of other ways encourage conservation.

Growing Presbyterian churches are more likely to be involved in environmental stewardship projects, according to Cynthia Woolever and Deborah Bruce, though only a small portion of PC(USA) congregations currently make a conscious ministry of it. They found growing Presbyterian congregations are much more likely to sponsor activities connected with the arts than are Presbyterian congregations generally.[9] Should these emphases be part of the new ecology? My guess is that they will soon be, if they are not already.

Study Questions

1. Are there emergent churches in your area? What is their appeal? In what ways can your church learn from them? In what ways is your congregation already an emergent church?
2. Do you and your congregation grow in faith from relating to people of other faiths? How and in what ways?
3. What place does environmental stewardship play in faith development? How does learning from the arts and from people involved in the various arts foster faith development?
4. What other elements in the new Presbyterian ecology can you identify from the cases and from your experience?

Chapter 11

A Sustainable Presbyterian Future

A new ecology now fosters faith development for members and leaders in many thriving Presbyterian congregations. Some elements in that new ecology—the ecumenical nature of it, the more inclusive assumptions regarding family, the reliance on digital methods of communication and social media as well as on print media, the necessary and intentional weaving of work and worship to form a coherent fabric, and the dependence on leadership that bubbles up from among many who belong to the congregations—all are obvious to those who take the effort to study them. A sustainable Presbyterian future relies on these, as well as on the constant ingredients in Presbyterian identity and culture—shared leadership, the authority of Scripture in all its richness, the secondary reliance on corporate confessions of faith, the commitment to disciplined discipleship, and so forth.

Other elements may also be contributing to sustainability—warm hospitality of Presbyterians toward believers in others of the living religions, for example. Support of the arts and stewardship of the environment and all God's creatures are two other ingredients probably in the mix. A sustainable future is being fed by the transformation of those who experience mission and evangelism firsthand and by the existence of creative new church developments, much as the traditional ecology was fed by the challenges of the various American frontiers and the missionary and martyr stories of meeting those challenges.

A new, or rather a re-formed sense of covenantal connections among Presbyterian Christians has replaced reliance on hierarchical authority or control from above that came to characterize the denominations of the early twentieth century. Members of both local congregations and denominational leaders affirm and foster it. That vocation and ministry bubbling up from distinctive congregational contexts presents a challenge for ruling elders, teaching elders, and others in positions at every level to exercise adaptive leadership and agency. Presbyterians are capable of meeting these challenges, however, for our identity and culture naturally foster shared leadership.

Many larger Presbyterian congregations are meeting the challenges thanks to their large number of members, competent pastoral leadership, and deep reserves of committed men and women from which to select and elect ruling elders and other lay leaders. Some are torn with issues of allegiance, questioning whether and in what fashion to remain in the PC(USA). But many Presbyterian congregations of all sizes are flourishing, seeking to be faithful, without feeling compromised by differences of opinion and differing emphases in mission within the denomination.

Moreover, many other Christian churches now bear more marks of Presbyterian and Reformed work and worship—shared leadership, balance between the authority of a flattened hierarchy and that of a congregation, expectation of a learned clergy, a balance of dignity and intimacy in worship, reliance on baptism and Lord's Supper as the two Christian sacraments, a balance of doing mercy and seeking justice in the wider world, and many more. So a Presbyterian future is, to some extent, being sustained outside the PC(USA) as well as within it.

But what about the average Presbyterian church? Is there a sustainable Presbyterian future for the average congregation of fewer than two hundred members—the one in a rural area or a rust belt state?

Consider Calypso Presbyterian.

Calypso Presbyterian Church: A Case Study

"You have arrived!" Wanda, my GPS, proclaims triumphantly after quite a solitary drive through the fields and forests of eastern North Carolina. I laugh out loud, for all I can see are a few empty buildings by a railroad track and some houses further down the street. One elder jokingly calls Calypso a "suburb of Mt. Olive," the nearest real town (population 4,800), about four miles away. Observing more carefully on second look, I can see the small church building on the other side of the train track berm. I cross the elevated track to join the ten adults and thirty-eight children engaged in vacation Bible school that day.

The children, ages five to twelve, some black, some Latino, but mostly white, come from the community and from nearby rural churches, as well as from the families of the congregation. They are following "Baobab Blast" VBS curriculum, published by Augsburg Fortress, a Lutheran press. Stuffed giraffes, lions, and monkeys decorate the learning space, along with carved figures and pictures from Africa.

Calypso Presbyterian Church is growing in membership (112 in 2010) and has active youth groups engaged in mission trips. Three adult Sunday school classes offer choices in formats. Every other Wednesday night during the school year, the church gathers for supper, educational programs, and meetings.

Youth groups draw junior and senior highs, and some families have joined as a result of the participation of their teenagers. Younger members participate in Wee Presbyterians, a junior choir, and they engage in study and local mission efforts. Adult and youth members participate in Habitat projects and supply and staff a food pantry. Cooperating with other congregations, they offer a regular dinner program for the poor. They give generously of their time and money for presbytery ministries.

The pastor, ruling elders, and members of Calypso Presbyterian credit one another for the congregational vitality. All agree their persistence in selecting first-call pastors over the decades has been positive. Pastors who have served Calypso point to the number of active leaders in the congregation that share responsibility and authority. They expect good pastoral care, biblically based sermons, well-run meetings, dignified-yet-intimate worship—all the marks of Presbyterian identity.

Retaining a Presbyterian Identity

Indeed Calypso Presbyterian Church, that small, rural congregation, thrives with a discernibly Presbyterian identity. It flourishes in the new ecology. It contributes in a healthy fashion to a healthy PC(USA). Pastor and ruling elders share leadership. Pastor Chris Currie tells it well. He speaks of a crisis his first day there, when a child in the congregation sustained a severe head injury in an automobile accident. Leaders in the congregation took responsibility for organizing assistance for the family as they watched over the child in an ICU in Greenville, some miles away. Currie explains, "They didn't need me as an organizer, or to help the family deal with the doctors. They needed me to be there, to pray with them, and to stand by them in times of trouble." Numbers of leaders simply did their share in a ministry that coalesced to meet that need and the other challenges faced.

Longtime members share the work and the leadership with those who joined more recently. They all practice a thick culture of hospitality—inviting everyone in the community and those in adjacent towns to come for vacation Bible school, fellowship, worship, and a part in caring for the community. They engage in God's mission globally and locally, instead of just focusing on themselves as a congregation.

Calypso Presbyterians have found a niche. They take pride in having called many pastors straight from seminary, as they called Chris Currie with his newly minted MDiv. They consider themselves a teaching church, as surely as do some large congregations with elaborate campuses. Perhaps finding a niche, a special mission, or expertise is necessary today, for those who study other sorts of institutions certainly advocate finding your niche.

When I wrote of the Calypso Presbyterian Church for a national publication, readers responded with words of admiration for that church and tales of other, similar Presbyterian congregations.[1] "Ah," a friend mused. "But can they keep it up?" He wondered if the Calypso congregation can maintain a Presbyterian identity and culture in the future. Do not the new ingredients in the ecology erode the Presbyterian identity toward one that is more generically ecumenical, more simplistic in employing the Bible for its own ends, less generous, less caring for literacy, and more complex treatments of ethical issues?

I responded that the Church of Jesus Christ proceeded fifteen hundred years, sometimes more faithfully, sometimes less, without an explicitly Presbyterian witness.

But I am quite sanguine that Calypso Presbyterian and its Presbyterian identity will endure and thrive.[2] Leaders and members of the Calypso Presbyterian Church are quite certain about the future. So are the other congregations studied in this project, even the ones that seem to be under stress for want of members or money.

In the final analysis, though, the determination of a sustainable Presbyterian future is not ours to make. In every congregation, in every age, the future belongs to God. The Holy Spirit quickens faith in believers. Our best-laid plans are just a measure of our hope and prayer. The initial chapter of our Foundations for Polity phrases our situation well:

> In affirming with the earliest Christians that Jesus is Lord, the Church confesses that he is its hope, and that the Church, as Christ's body, is bound to his authority and thus free to live in the lively, joyous reality of the grace of God. (F-1.0204)

My prayer is that Presbyterians will grow in God's grace and continue faithfully to fulfill our part in the many-faceted Christian Church, the body of Christ.

Study Questions

1. What makes Calypso Presbyterian Church distinctively Presbyterian? What can we learn from its work and worship?
2. How does your congregation help members and other Presbyterians witness faithfully in the world today?
3. How do you phrase your prayers for God's will to be done in the PC(USA)? In your congregation? In the world?

Notes

PREFACE

1. See Bill Leonard, *God's Last and Only Hope: The Fragmentation of the Southern Baptist Convention* (Grand Rapids: Eerdmans, 1990). Leonard uses the phrase ironically. On the holiness movement, including Presbyterian involvement, Jean Miller Schmidt offered a succinct essay, "Holiness and Perfection," in the *Encyclopedia of the American Religious Experience*, ed. Charles H. Lippy and Peter W. Williams (New York: Charles Scribner's Sons, 1988), 2:813–29. See also Edith L. Blumhofer, et al., eds. *Pentecostal Currents in American Protestantism* (Urbana: University of Illinois Press, 1999), and Donald W. Dayton, *Theological Roots of Pentecostalism* (Metuchen, NJ: Scarecrow Press, 1987).

2. *The Constitution of the Presbyterian Church (U.S.A.)*, Part I, *Book of Confessions* (Louisville, KY: Office of the General Assembly, Presbyterian Church (U.S.A.), 2004), 10.4.

3. Ibid., 6.143–.144.

4. Pew Research Center Publications, "The Decline of Marriage and Rise of New Families," November 18, 2010, http://pewresearch.org/pubs/1802/decline-marriage-rise-new-families.

5. James Davison Hunter, *To Change the World* (Oxford: University Press, 2010), 14.

6. Sharon Youngs, "Presbyteries of the Presbyterian Church (U.S.A.) Have Approved a New Form of Government," June 7, 2011, http://www.pcusa.org/news/2011/6/7/presbyteries-presbyterian-church-us-have-approved-/.

CHAPTER 1: PRESBYTERIANS TOTTERING AND THRIVING

1. Russell D. Moore, "Where Have All the Presbyterians Gone?" *Wall Street Journal*, February 4, 2011. Dr. Moore is Dean of Southern Seminary, Louisville, KY. The op-ed piece, for which Moore said an editor chose the headline singling out Presbyterians, admonished all denominational leaders to focus on the Christian Gospel.

2. Milton J Coalter John M. Mulder, and Louis B. Weeks, eds., *The Re-Forming Tradition: Presbyterians and Mainstream Protestantism* (Louisville,

KY: Westminster/John Knox Press, 1992), 67 for a summary. Current figures are from Research Services, PC(USA), current membership, tagline of Presbyterian Church (USA) Web site, December 9, 2011, says 2.3M but "2010 Summaries of Statistics" says 2M "active members" (http://www.pcusa.org/resource/2010-summaries-statistics-comparative-summaries).

3. For a succinct account, see Louis Weeks, "Presbyterianism," in *Encyclopedia of the American Religious Experience: Studies of Traditions and Movements*, vol. 1, ed. Charles H. Lippy and Peter W. Williams (New York: Charles Scribner's Sons, 1988), 499–510. Volume 1 of the three-volume encyclopedia gives similar accounts of the other major Christian streams in American life.

4. Among the most accurate and extensive are Lefferts A. Loetscher, *A Brief History of the Presbyterians* (Philadelphia: Westminster Press, 1983); Leonard J. Trinterud, *The Forming of an American Tradition: A Re-Examination of Colonial Presbyterianism* (Philadelphia: Westminster Press, 1949); Walter Lee Lingle and John W. Kuykendall, *Presbyterians: Their History and Beliefs* (Atlanta: John Knox, 1978); Ernest Trice Thompson, *Presbyterians in the South*, 3 vols. (Atlanta: John Knox Press, 1963–1973); and Robert Ellis Thompson, *A History of the Presbyterian Churches in the United States* (New York: The Christian Literature Co., 1895).

5. Milton J Coalter, John M. Mulder, and Louis B. Weeks, eds., *The Presbyterian Presence: The Twentieth-Century Experience* (Louisville, KY: Westminster/John Knox Press, 1990–1992). There were seven volumes in this series.

6. *The Constitution of the Presbyterian Church (U.S.A.)*, Part II, *Book of Order* (Louisville, KY: Office of the General Assembly, Presbyterian Church (U.S.A.), 2011).

7. Craig Dykstra and James Hudnut-Beumler, "The National Organizational Structures of Protestant Denominations: An Invitation to a Conversation," in *The Organizational Revolution: Presbyterians and Mainstream Denominationalism*, ed. Milton J Coalter, John M. Mulder, and Louis B. Weeks (Louisville, KY: Westminster/John Knox Press, 1992), 307–20.

8. A summary of the insight is available in Coalter, Mulder, and Weeks, *Re-forming Tradition*, 191–224.

9. For a summary, see ibid., 91–116.

10. Ibid., 94. Originally from Louis Weeks and William Fogleman, "A Two-Church Hypothesis," *Presbyterian Outlook* 172 (March 26, 1990): 8-10.

CHAPTER 2: PRESBYTERIAN IDENTITY AND CULTURE

1. *The Constitution of the Presbyterian Church (U.S.A.)*, Part I, *Book of Confessions* (Louisville, KY: Office of the General Assembly, Presbyterian Church (U.S.A.), 2004), 6.109.

2. Note it comes third, after vows concerning the Christian faith of the elder and a promise to "accept the Scriptures of the Old and New Testaments to be, by the power of the Holy Spirit, the unique and authoritative witness to Jesus Christ."

3. Jack Marcum, Coordinator of Research Services, PC(USA), shared these statistics:

**Trends among Presbyterian Members in Self-Reported
Theological Perspective**

Q. Which of the following best describes your current stand on theological issues?	Year of Survey					
	1993	1996	1999	2002	2005	2008
Very conservative	5%	8%	5%	5%	6%	6%
Conservative	27%	31%	33%	33%	35%	28%
Moderate	51%	48%	47%	43%	40%	41%
Liberal	14%	11%	12%	14%	14%	18%
Very liberal	3%	3%	3%	3%	5%	7%

Source: Presbyterian Panel surveys. Reprinted by permission of Research Services, Presbyterian Church (U.S.A.).

4. Deborah Tannen, *The Argument Culture: Stopping America's War of Words* (New York: Ballentine Books, 1998).

5. Borrowing from Clifford Geertz, "I . . . use the word 'culture' to mean a web of significance spun among interactive people, involving an intricate system of sending and receiving meaning within a human community. I use 'identity' to mean the explicit recognition of what may be an implicit ethos and a tacit culture, an intentional legitimator of a culture." Louis B. Weeks, "Presbyterian Culture: Views from 'the Edge' " in *Beyond Establishment: Protestant Identity in a Post-Protestant Age*, ed. Jackson Carroll and Wade Clark Roof (Louisville, KY: Westminster/John Knox Press, 1993), 309.

6. Ibid., 316.

7. Ibid., 315.

8. Ibid., 316.

CHAPTER 3: A NEW PRESBYTERIAN ECOLOGY

1. Milton J Coalter, John M. Mulder, and Louis B. Weeks, eds., *The Re-Forming Tradition: Presbyterians and Mainstream Protestantism* (Louisville, KY: Westminster/John Knox Press, 1992), 191–222.

2. Milton J Coalter, John M. Mulder, Louis B. Weeks, *Vital Signs: The Promise of Mainstream Protestantism* (Grand Rapids: Eerdmans, 1996), 77, 78.

3. Wade Clark Roof, *Spiritual Marketplace: Baby Boomers and the Remaking of American Religion* (Princeton: Princeton University Press, 1999), 294.

4. Ibid., 294–314.

5. Robert Wuthnow, *After the Baby Boomers: How Twenty- and Thirty-Somethings Are Shaping the Future of American Religion* (Princeton: Princeton University Press, 2007), 13–17, and the implications are explored in subsequent chapters.

6. Nancy Tatom Ammerman, *Pillars of Faith: American Congregations and Their Partners* (Berkeley: University of California Press, 2005), 206. A note of

general indebtedness to her work for perceiving the new ecology has prevailed more broadly in American denominations.

CHAPTER 4: INSTITUTIONS AND ELEMENTS COMPRISING THE NEW ECOLOGY

1. See the Web site for First Presbyterian Church, Binghamton, NY, http:// unitedpresbyterian.org/mission.html. First Presbyterian and West Presbyterian did merge in September 2011 to form the United Presbyterian Church of Binghamton, NY. The mission efforts continue in a church with two campuses.

2. See the Web site for Christ Presbyterian Church, Edina, MN, http://www .cpconline.org/index.php?content=home.

3. Ibid., http://www.cpconline.org/index.php?content=growinghope.

4. Ibid., http://www.cpconline.org/uploaded_files/gowinghope.pdf.

5. Milton J Coalter, John M. Mulder, and Louis B. Weeks, *Vital Signs: The Promise of Mainstream Protestantism* (Grand Rapids: Eerdmans, 1996), 79.

6. Toni Montgomery, "Building Community, Box by Box," *Presbyterian News Service*, November 12, 2010, http://www.pcusa.org/news/2010/11/12/building -community-box-box/.

7. Carol Howard Merritt, *Tribal Church: Ministering to the Missing Generation* (Herndon, VA: Alban Institute Press, 2009), 85.

8. Ibid.

9. See the Web site for Bend Youth Collective, Bend, OR, http://www.bend fpc.org. See *Presbyterians Today* (June 2011): 36.

CHAPTER 5: INTEGRITY AND AGENCY IN PRESBYTERIAN WORSHIP AND WORK

1. John Buchanan, "The Reformed Theological Tradition: A Way of Being Christian," in *Presbyterians Being Reformed*, ed. Robert H. Bullock, Jr. (Louisville, KY: Geneva Press, 2006), 46. Buchanan has provided this insight in numerous speeches and sermons.

2. Ronald Heifetz, Alexander Grashow, and Marty Linsky, *The Practice of Adaptive Leadership: Tools and Tactics for Changing Your Organization and the World* (Cambridge: Harvard Business Press, 2009), 14.

3. Louis B. Weeks, *All for God's Glory: Redeeming Church Scutwork* (Herndon, VA: Alban Institute Press, 2009), 124-25. One worship service has been added since 2009.

4. Nancy Tatom Ammerman, *Pillars of Faith: American Congregations and Their Partners* (Berkeley: University of California Press, 2005); Diana Butler Bass, *The Practicing Congregation: Imagining a New Old Church* (New York: Simon and Schuster, 2000); Diana Butler Bass, *Christianity for the Rest of Us: How the Neighborhood Church Is Transforming the Faith* (San Francisco: Harper, 2007). General indebtedness for their arguments and their sanguine perspectives on the mainline churches.

5. Gary Gunderson with Larry Pray, *Leading Causes of Life* (Memphis, TN: The Center of Excellence in Faith and Health, 2006), 107.

6. Richard L. Morrill, *Strategic Leadership: Integrating Strategy and Leadership in Colleges and Universities* (Lanham, MD: Rowman & Littlefield Publishers, 2007), 8. Morrill, a Presbyterian ethicist, is writing appropriately for a secular audience.

7. Heifetz, Grashow, and Linsky, *Practice of Adaptive Leadership,* 14.

8. Ronald Heifetz, *Leadership without Easy Answers* (Cambridge: Harvard University Press, 1998), 252–63. This is the best discussion of the concept, though it is treated in every Heifetz book.

9. Leslie Scanlon, "Out of the Ashes: A Charlotte Church is 'the Miracle on Fifth Street,'" *The Presbyterian Outlook* (January 10, 2011): 17–18.

10. See the Web site for Elmwood Presbyterian Church, East Orange, West Orange, and Newark, NJ, http://www.elmwoodchurchnj.org/cmcms/harambee _ministry.html.

11. Jill M. Hudson, *When Better Isn't Enough: Evaluation Tools for the 21st-Century Church* (Herndon, VA: Alban Institute Press, 2004), 74.

12. Jack Haberer, *Godviews: The Convictions That Drive Us and Divide Us* (Louisville, KY: Geneva Press, 2001), 156–59.

CHAPTER 6: PRESBYTERIAN CONGREGATIONAL RESOURCES

1. Scott Thumma and Warren Bird, *The Other 80 Percent: Turning Your Church's Spectators into Active Participants* (San Francisco: Jossey-Bass, 2011).

2. Louis B. Weeks, "American Protestants Today: Thriving, Tottering, and Tinkering Together on the Mainline," *The Journal of Presbyterian History* 88, no. 1 (2010): 3.

3. See the Web site for Brown Memorial Park Avenue Presbyterian Church, Baltimore, MD, http://www.browndowntown.org/ and Andrew Foster Connors, "Testimony for Mission in the Next Church" (presentation at NEXT Conference, Second Presbyterian Church, Indianapolis, IN, February 28, 2011).

4. See the Web site for Menlo Park Presbyterian Church, Menlo Park, CA, http://mppc.org/serve/world.

CHAPTER 7: DENOMINATIONAL RESOURCES

1. Gradye Parsons, blog, "Extraordinary," August 4, 2011.

2. Carmen Fowler, The Layman Online, March 3, 2011, http://www.layman .org/news.aspx?article=28139.

3. "No 2011 Pension Experience Apportionment, BOP Says," Presbyterian News Service, March 14, 2011.

4. Janet Tuck, "Aftermath: Tuscaloosa Churches, PDA Committed to Post-Tornado Rebuilding," August 5, 2011, http://www.pcusa.org/news/2011/8/5/aftermath/.

5. *Reutkemeier v. Nolte*, 179 Iowa 342, 161 N.W. 290 (February 14, 1917).

6. Nancy Tatom Ammerman, *Pillars of Faith: American Congregations and Their Partners* (Berkeley: University of California Press, 2005); Diana Butler Bass,

The Practicing Congregation: Imagining a New Old Church (New York: Simon and Schuster, 2000), 247.

7. Ibid.

CHAPTER 8: PRESBYTERIAN SEMINARIES AND COLLEGES

1. See the Web site for University Presbyterian Church, Chapel Hill, NC, http://www.upc.org/convergence.aspx.

2. See the Web site for University Presbyterian Church, Seattle, WA, www.upc.org/umin.aspx.

CHAPTER 9: VOICING OUR FAITH AS PRESBYTERIANS

1. See the Web site for Ormond Beach Presbyterian Church, Ormond Beach, FL, http://ormondbeachpc.org/Video.html.

2. See the Vital Churches Institute Web site for more about this program, http://vitalchurchesinstitute.com/pages/acts-16-5.

3. N. Graham Standish, *Becoming a Blessed Church: Forming a Church of Spiritual Purpose, Presence, and Power* (Herndon, VA: Alban Institute Press, 2004). See also his more recent *Humble Leadership: Being Radically Open to God's Guidance and Grace* (Herndon, VA: Alban Institute Press, 2007).

4. http://ngrahamstandish.org/site/comments_about_graham.htm. See Graham Standish Web site for more testimonies.

5. For information on the books, the program, the coaching, and other resources, see the Web site, Grace Net, www.gracenet.info. Martha Grace Reese is president of that nonprofit corporation.

6. See the Web site, Anthony B. Robinson, http://www.anthonybrobinson.com/. Also see the Congregational Leadership Northwest Web site, http://clnorthwest.org/. Tony is the president of that nonprofit.

7. See the Web site of Pioneer Memorial Presbyterian Church, Salon, OH, http://pioneersolon.org/default.aspx.

8. Kerri Peterson-Davis, "I Wonder Where This Road Will Take Us," http://www.revkpd.com/.

9. Foster H. Shannon, *Why Are These Presbyterian Churches Growing? The Story of Fifteen Thriving Presbyterian Churches* (Alhambra, CA: Green Leaf Press, 2009).

10. See the Web site of Bethel Presbyterian Church, Kingston, TN, http://www.bethelpcusa.org/worship.php.

CHAPTER 10: EMERGING POSSIBILITIES

1. See the Web site of Broad Street Ministry, Philadelphia, PA, http://broadstreetministry.org/about.

2. Don Allen, *Barefoot in the Church: Sensing the Authentic through the House Church* (Atlanta: John Knox Press, 1972).

3. See Louis Weeks, "All for God's Glory," *Presbyterians Today,* 57-62.

4. Annie Lamont, *Plan B: Further Thoughts on Faith* (New York: Riverhead Books, 2005), 15.

5. Robert D. Putnam and David E. Campbell, *American Grace: How Religion Divides and Unites Us* (New York: Simon and Schuster, 2010), 519-40; quote is from 526.

6. Robert Wuthnow, *America and the Challenge of Religious Diversity* (Princeton: Princeton University Press, 2005), 139.

7. Putnam and Campbell, *American Grace*, 531.

8. Ibid., 537.

9. Deborah Bruce and Cynthia Woolever, *A Field Guide to Presbyterian Congregations: Who's Going Where and Why* (Louisville, KY: Westminster John Knox Press, 2010), 20. Also see their pamphlet, "The U.S. Congregational Life Survey: Fastest Growing Presbyterian Churches" (Louisville, KY: Research Services, 2004).

CHAPTER 11: A SUSTAINABLE PRESBYTERIAN FUTURE

1. Louis B. Weeks, "Calypso Presbyterian Church," *Christian Century*, (December 14, 2010): 12.

2. Can we learn from evolutionary theory in this as well? Might the ingredients in the new ecology even enrich Presbyterian identity and culture? A recent article in the *American Naturalist* offers notes and comments on findings that contradict Darwinian orthodoxy regarding what scientists call *congeneric species*. Charles Darwin postulated that alien species similar to native flora and fauna would not flourish in competition with native species already part of the ecology. Australian scientists now find that introduced species of amphibians actually thrive and enrich the ecosystems they migrate to join. Reid Tingley, Benjamin L. Phillips, and Richard Shine, "Establishment Success of Introduced Amphibians Increases in the Presence of Congeneric Species," *American Naturalist* 177 (March 2011), 382–88.

CPSIA information can be obtained at www.ICGtesting.com
Printed in the USA
LVOW050922030612

284400LV00004B/3/P

9 780664 503192